ENDORSEMENTS

"Searching for Mambia is a life-changer! Paul and Jennifer will inspire you to lean into God, embrace His adventure for your life, and become braver, more courageous, and more compassionate toward all the peoples around the world. If you are tired of the rat-race, ho-hum, daily grind and you long for something more, read this inspiring story of an 'ordinary' family who took God up on an 'extraordinary' opportunity. God may have an equally inspiring journey in store for you too! This book is a page-turner and must read for anyone who wants all God has for them and those they love."

- Pam and Bill Farrel, Co-Directors of Love-Wise ministries, international speakers, and authors of Men Are Like Waffles, Women Are Like Spaghetti, plus more than 50 other books

"At the end of the day, as followers of Jesus, the question is: will we follow where He leads? And will we follow with a heart of faith? Paul and Jenn are very normal people, like the rest of us. People who just keep saying yes to God. This book is a story of that. But not only that, it's a story of how we too can open our lives to obedience to God that starts feeling like real faith in a real God who is at work redeeming the whole world. May this book give you the courage and the hope to step into your own Mambia."

- Dave Lomas, Pastor of Reality San Francisco and author of The Truest Thing About You

"Searching for Mambia recounts the spiritual, intellectual, and practical journey that Paul and Jenn Prelle traveled in their quest to hear and follow God's missionary calling on their life. Coupled with the reflective questions you'll find at the end of each chapter, this book can help you think through and hopefully, see more clearly, God's unique calling for your own life and ministry."

- Larry Osbourne, Pastor of North Coast Church and Author of multiple books including Sticky Teams and Lead Like A Shepherd

SEARCHING FOR MAMBIA

SEARCHING FOR MAMBIA

DISCOVERING ADVENTURE WHEN GOD LEADS

PAUL AND JENNIFER PRELLE

Printed in the United States of America

First Printing, 2019

ISBN 978-1-0781-6067-4

Published by Paul Prelle Vista, CA 92083

www.onejeremiah.com

DEDICATION

This book is dedicated to Ibrahim Delamou. He was the only son of Pepe Delamou but passed away just before his 7th birthday. We miss you and can't wait to see you again in heaven.

To all those who have given so much, not only to the ministry, but also to us personally, even when we forgot to say thanks.

To our parents for the upbringing and all the opportunities you gave us.

To the people who have continually labored in prayer even when we weren't aware.

To Pam and Bill Farrell, without whom, this book probably never would have come to completion.

FOREWORD

What would you say if I told you that I had a dream that caused my family to move to Africa? What would you say if I told you in that dream, God gave me the name of a specific village? What would you say if I told you my husband and I packed up and moved to Guinea with our children, Selah, who was four and Cedar, who was two at the time? Would you call me crazy? Well, that is what some people said and it marked the beginning of a journey and a new lifestyle that would always be labeled as crazy. What follows is my husband's account of this amazing journey, along with some entries from my personal journal interjected throughout. We hope that you enjoy this book and more importantly, that you are inspired to walk in obedience and step out in faith to see what the Lord might do in and through your life. It just takes a mustard seed planted in the right soil!

Jennifer Prelle

CHAPTER ONE

NOT A MISSIONARY

Y ou're nuts! You can't take your four-year-old and two-year-old and move to a third world country in West Africa." This was the reaction we got from many people before we moved to Guinea, West Africa in the summer of 2007. It was also our own reaction when we first heard the call of God on our lives. It seemed so impossible and unreasonable, especially for people like us...

My wife and I met at Simpson University, a Christian college in Northern California. Despite being a part of a great school that was focused on reaching the lost world with the gospel, we never wanted to be overseas missionaries, and I mean NEVER! My limited view of a missionary was that they were strange people who just did not fit very well into society. They seemed socially awkward and therefore, good candidates to just start over in another country! Looking back now, I realize that much of what I was seeing was the difference living in another culture can have on the individual and I feel horrible for my judgmental perspective.

During our time at Simpson, my wife and I both had ideals for a future spouse. Included on that list for both of us was "not a missionary." In fact, Jenn remembers asking me during our dating time if I wanted to be a missionary. When I responded that I did not, her reply was, "Good. Me neither". It is the honest truth. We just did not have a desire for missions. Now please do not misunderstand me. We definitely thought evangelism was important. We knew that it was God's desire to reach the lost, but neither of us felt comfortable or gifted in that area. My first experience with missions was going to Scotland with a drama team in the summer of 1997. I went because Scotland sounded awesome. I also loved doing drama and was excited to learn and perform more skits. It was an incredible trip and I saw God move in ways I never could have imagined. I came away from that experience with a vision and desire to reach local youth with some sort of activity center. At the time, it did not do too much to change my view on overseas work, however, I can see now that it was a big step in the direction that God would eventually take me.

In 1999, I was married to my beautiful wife, Jennifer. We were both planning on being elementary teachers but God had other plans that would put ours on hold for the time. Our first stop as a married couple was Bakersfield, CA. The plan was to obtain our teaching credential at a California State University, and we needed some place where the cost of living was low. Bakersfield fit the bill. We had quite a rough start as we struggled to gain employment. My first job involved selling books, lotions, clocks and other products door-to-door. This was a horrible thing to do while dressed in a suit and tie walking the streets where summer temperatures often rose to over 100 degrees!

A few months later, God graciously opened a door for me to begin serving as a youth pastor. For the next seven years, we thoroughly enjoyed being a part of Westbrook Chapel in Bakersfield. In addition to leading the Junior High ministry there, I was also given the position of Church Administrator. The relationships we made at that church made our time in Bakersfield worthwhile and some of them continue to be our strongest friendships to this day.

"Having come from a fairly humble start, it was beginning to feel like we were finally making it in life. We were living the American dream."

During this time working at a church, my view on missions did not change too much. I definitely saw a value in reaching the lost in the local community, but I had bought into a lie when it came to traveling overseas. My thought was that it was a waste of time and money. Why would we spend thousands of dollars and multiple years training people to send them to a country where Christians were already living? In fact, I reasoned, many of these countries were also sending missionaries to America! It's much more practical to minister in your own country. This was another view that would change after becoming a missionary myself and seeing the value of such personal sacrifice as well as the impact on those being visited. Although Kern County was certainly not our first choice in places to settle down, we quickly fell in love with the people there and began to get comfortable.

As well as having a great job, we had recently purchased our first home. It was a lovely, three-bedroom house that. With the help of my dad, we had also completed a large addition to make room for our growing family. Our daughter, Selah was born in the summer of 2003 and just under two years later we had our son, Cedar. Besides that, I had recently purchased a PT Cruiser that I absolutely loved! Having come from a fairly humble start, it was beginning to feel like we were finally making it in life. We were living the American dream. Believe it or not, we actually had a white picket fence in the front yard as well! We enjoyed our "picture perfect" lives and had no plans of doing anything differently... No plans that is, until one life-changing evening in July 2006.

YOUR SEARCH...

What experiences or situations has God used in your life to grow or shape you but you did not realize until later in life?

What circumstances in your life right now do not make sense?

Ask God to help you trust Him with the things you do not understand, knowing that if you allow Him, He will use them as a benefit to you later on.

"And we know that in all things God works for the good of those who love him, who have been called according to His purpose." – Romans 8:28

CHAPTER TWO

MAKE ME READY

The events that took place in July 2006 should be prefaced with the work that God began to do in us during the summer of 2004. During that summer, our church went through a very challenging time. On June 21st, we lost a precious little two-year old girl named Chloe. She drowned in her backyard pool. It was very difficult to watch her parents and older siblings go through that time. Less than two months later, one of our junior high students lost her older brother in an automobile accident. Once again, we struggled to find words to comfort our friends in the midst of their tragedy.

Shortly after these two sudden deaths, we lost someone else whom we had been very close to. Danielle had been a student in our youth group. At the tender age of 17, she was killed in a car accident, minutes from her home. It was a devastating time for everyone and, along with the pain, we were challenged to grow in new ways. So many began to question God. What was He doing and why? For me personally, these tragedies made me realize the frailty of life and made me think more about the return of Christ. I had always heard that Jesus could come back at any time, but until then, I never really believed it. As local and world events brought to mind the last days that Jesus spoke of, I came to strongly believe that Jesus' return was indeed very soon.

"For in just a very little while, 'He who is coming will come and will not delay." – Hebrews 10:37

This new conviction for me, brought up a pressing question. With the return of our Savior quickly approaching, what did that mean for my life personally? As I struggled with that question, it became very clear to me that I should be sharing the Good News of the Gospel with many more people. If I really believed that the information I held could save lives, I needed to be doing something about it. I just knew in my heart that there must be something more. I wanted to do more than just live the comfortable American life.

"My comfortable life was stifling my relationship with my Savior because I had forgotten how much I really needed Him."

Another one of the lessons that God was teaching me, was the value of suffering. I know that this is not an easy concept to swallow, but pain really can bring more growth than smooth sailing. One Sunday, as I taught about this issue to the Junior High group, I realized that I needed to experience more personal suffering in order to really grow closer to God. My comfortable life was stifling my relationship with my Savior because I had forgotten how much I really needed Him. As I stood at the pulpit, I said to the students (but more to God), "Bring on the trials. I want to grow. I want to know more about God and be closer to Him."

It was the first time I had ever prayed something like this and I really meant it. As soon as I had spoken those words out loud, my cell phone began vibrating in my pocket. Still standing at the pulpit, I pulled out the phone and looked at the screen. The call was from my wife. I set the phone on the podium and continued with the sermon. After the service was over, I listened to my voicemail. My heart raced as I listened to the message. In a shaky voice, my wife explained that she had just arrived at our house. When she got inside, she noticed that our house had been ransacked. Someone had broken into our home while we were at church. Things were missing, mattresses were flipped over and the back door was still wide open. "WOW!" I said to myself. "That happened a lot quicker than I thought!" Had I not been ready for the trial, I would have responded much differently that morning. I would have been angry and fearful instead of completely at peace.

Through the trial, we saw God's amazing protection over us. My daughter had walked into the house before my wife and quite possibly scared the criminals away. We praise the Lord that He protected her. The police explained that the criminals were searching our house for weapons, jewelry and money. They had pulled out drawers, looked through our closet, and even under our mattress. In the end though, they only walked away with a piggy bank containing $20-$30 dollars and a small MP3 player that was on the fritz. Somehow, they managed to leave an envelope with about $60 that was sitting right next to the piggy bank, another envelope with about $300 in one of the drawers that was pulled out! They also left our computer, DVD player, TV and other valuables. Though most of our valuables were spared, I had to ask myself, "If they had taken everything, would I still praise God?" Would I be able to echo Job's sentiment when he blessed the Lord even when he had lost everything? This was one more step towards learning to trust God with everything.

"Naked I came from my mother's womb, and naked I will depart. The Lord gave and the Lord has taken away; may the name of the Lord be praised." – Job 1:21

"Consider it pure joy, my brothers and sisters, whenever you face trials of many kinds, because you know that the testing of your faith produces perseverance. Let perseverance finish its work so that you may be mature and complete, not lacking anything." – James 1:2-4

God also began to work with me in the area of Spirit-led obedience. I began to realize the importance of not only listening to Him, but also in setting aside time for Him to speak and then stepping out in faith, even when it did not make sense. One example of this came shortly after I failed to be obedient to His call in another area.

I was at church when I saw a homeless man riding a bike through the parking lot. I felt strongly that I was supposed to offer him some money, but I hesitated and let the opportunity pass me by. That following weekend, I was at the church again, this time for a men's prayer breakfast. After a short teaching, we began our time of prayer. After only a few minutes with my small prayer group, I again felt an urging that I was supposed to get up and leave the room. This time I decided to put the feeling to the test and determine if perhaps it was from God. I left the room and headed out of the parking lot in my car. As I left, I again felt a prodding to turn the opposite direction that I would normally have gone. A short way down the road, I suddenly saw the same homeless man that I had seen earlier that week, riding his bike on the side of the road. I praised the Lord for giving me another opportunity to walk in obedience to Him! The man thanked me for the money that I gave to him and went on his way. There was nothing amazing or miraculous about the encounter, but I left with a stronger conviction and encouragement to act whenever I felt the Holy Spirit's leading in my life. It was a strong reminder that sometimes God calls us to do things that do not seem to make sense from our perspective. Perhaps it is just a chance to become better acquainted with His voice.

In the early part of 2006, I received a book from a good friend of mine, Dave. The book that he gave me was called, *The Heavenly Man*. It told the amazing story of a Chinese believer named Brother Yun. After reading the book, I had a real burning to be used in a new way by the Lord. I was not sure where it was all leading but I knew that I did not want to continue living the same way. I had not considered moving out of Bakersfield at that point, but I really wanted to live a life of true sacrifice. Since it was very important to me that Jenn and I were on the same page, I kept encouraging her to read the book. My thought was that she would experience the same change of heart and gain a similar passion by reading the book. She told me that she would read it, but she continually put it off. I started to get a little frustrated because I wanted to do more than just share what I was feeling. I wanted her to have the same conviction on her own. Little did I know at that time, but God had already been working on her heart as well. It should not have been a surprise that He did not need me to be the Holy Spirit to my wife!

Jenn will tell you that her journey can also be traced back to that difficult summer of 2004. It was then that she came to the realization that life is short and that it does not belong to us. In October, following those deaths that summer, she went on a women's retreat to Hume Lake and really began working through these thoughts. As a mom, she struggled with the thought that there are no guarantees in life. She realized that she was no different from these other moms who lost their children that summer. It very easily could have been her. She was struck by the fact that the only guarantee in this life is Jesus Christ. It was a good heart check and a huge turning point in her life. Towards the end of the retreat, she bought a plaque from the gift store that hung on our daughter's wall for years to come. The plaque said "Love like there is no tomorrow" and it served as a reminder that life is short, and we do not know what tomorrow holds. Each day is a gift from God, and we need to cherish every moment. This deeper understanding of life here on Earth helped her grasp the concept that this life is temporal and belongs to the Lord.

In May 2006, we went to Hawaii on a family vacation. It was there that Jenn began feeling from the Lord that there was more He wanted from her life. It was this stirring up inside that got her thinking, praying and listening. She felt like God might be prompting us to be missionaries, but she wasn't sure and since she did not want that, she sure wasn't going to say anything to me! She held these thoughts inside until one night, only a few months later.

YOUR SEARCH...

Has there been a moment in your life when God asked you to do something that did not make sense? What was it and how did it turn out?

What are you doing now or what can you do to provide the Holy Spirit the opportunity to speak into your life?

If you are too busy to be interrupted by God, make a commitment to carve out some time to hear from Him.

"Show me your ways, Lord, teach me your paths. Guide me in your truth and teach me, for you are God my Savior, and my hope is in you all day long." – Psalm 25:4-5

CHAPTER THREE
NIGHT VISION

It was July 1st, 2006. Jenn and I watched a movie that night. The choice was a little known film called, *In the Time of Butterflies*. The movie was based on the true story of sisters who fought for freedom against an unjust government. (SPOILER ALERT! Skip the next two sentences if you don't want to know how the movie ends.) At the end of the movie they all died! Through their death, however, they helped to bring about the freedom that they had desired. It was far from a blockbuster, (in other words, don't tell someone that we recommended it!) but it got Jenn and me talking afterwards. I told her how it seemed like such an honor to be able to die for something that you believe in. It was not something temporary, like a political power that I was referring to, but to the journey of a true disciple who changes the world for Jesus Christ through their life and their death.

"It only took a moment for me to become convinced that if we did not move soon, we would never take that step."

"I could see us becoming missionaries someday", Jenn said offhanded. As soon as she said it, I heard the word "GO" in my heart. It was not loud but it was distinct. My heart raced and I got goosebumps all over. Immediately, I felt a sense of fear and then an overwhelming peace. I responded, "That's it! That is exactly what God wants. He wants us to be missionaries." To my surprise, she said that she believed God had been trying to show her the same thing. She had not said anything though because she knew we would have to act on it.

As we began to talk, I realized what a struggle she was going through. She gave every excuse in the book for why we could not go. Her mom and sister had recently moved to Bakersfield to be around us. We had done so much work on our house and were not ready to part with it. Our kids were so young to take from their stable environment. We loved our church and enjoyed working in the ministry there. We had no training and very little experience. The reasons went on and on. They were good reasons. Good in the sense that they sounded wise from a human perspective. Reasons that I believe have kept many from stepping out in faith. Her thought was that we would probably become missionaries someday, but just not now. In her mind, it was the wrong time. Perhaps God was preparing us for when our children moved off to college.

It only took a moment for me to become convinced that if we did not move soon, we would never take that step. It would just become a story that we told to others someday; a story similar to the one that some people shared with us before we made the move. "Yeah, we were almost missionaries years ago," they would say. "We felt like that was what God wanted, but it just didn't work out."

During our conversation, Jenn mentioned a few times that it would be too overwhelming to sell everything we had and just move with our kids to Africa. I stopped her. "I don't want to go to Africa," I said. I knew we were being called to go someplace but I did not want to go to a foreign country. I had some masculine, renegade idea that we would buy a motorhome and head across the United States sharing the gospel with everyone we met. Oh well, I thought. I'll help her sort out the location details later. For now, let's just focus on the going.

We went round and round for a few hours. Our discussion was not as much with each other as it was with the Lord. Just past midnight, we spent some time in prayer before going to sleep. We asked God to show us clearly what He wanted us to do with our lives. It was a long night and neither of us slept very well. My body was pumping with adrenaline as I realized that our lives were about to change forever. Whatever we decided, I knew that things would never be the same.

Jenn was a wreck that night. She will tell you that it was one of the hardest nights of her life. Similarly to me, she spent the night tossing and turning, but for her, the reasons were much different. She felt like vomiting because everything seemed out of her control. As a very organized person, she definitely relies on her routines. To be thinking about doing something like moving, just stressed her out. Many thoughts raced through her head, but the odd thing was that they were all answered by the Lord. I did not have to reason with her or say much of anything. Her turmoil was not between her and I. It was between her and the Lord. Deep down, she knew that the Lord wanted us to do this.

The next morning Jenn went into the office and got on the computer. A few minutes later I heard her calling for me. When I went into the office, she was sitting at the computer in tears. "What's wrong?" I asked her. She explained that after we prayed the night before, she had fallen asleep and God had given her some kind of vision. Before I get into the details, please understand that this is not commonplace for us. Neither of us have had what we could call a vision before or since this time. We seek God's guidance regularly but are not accustomed to hearing Him speak audibly or give us signs and wonders. This night was a totally unique experience for both of us.

In this vision, she saw a picture, like on a map, and the word "mambia". Not knowing what the word was, she typed it on an internet search engine. The second thing on the list was an entry that read like this: VILLAGE OF MAMBIA, WEST AFRICA RECEIVES THE GOSPEL FOR THE FIRST TIME IN 2002. She was blown away! The name of the village was spelled exactly like it was in her dream. I was shocked as well. It was not very exciting to see that it was a village in Africa but I knew I could not argue with what God was doing. We realized then just how big our God was and knew that He was going to show us exactly what we needed in order to walk in obedience with what He had for our future.

Looking back, it is also incredible to think that, as far as I can determine, there is only one Mambia in the whole world. When you consider how many cities have other places with the same name, it is incredible to see that God did not allow us to experience any confusion in that area. Even recently, we have done internet searches and there is little to no information regarding this small town in Guinea. The other day, my wife and I were commenting on how amazing it is that it was a location. The chances are actually not that high. If you don't believe me, just try it yourself. Think of any random set of letters that might be a word. Do a search for that word. Most likely you are going to end up with a person's name, an autocorrect for something else or some kind of disease! In our opinion, finding this place was nothing short of a miracle.

For Jenn, seeing the word "Mambia" in her dream was exactly what she needed. God is amazing and so perfect that He would show her the word Mambia. He knew how impossible it would be to just accept it from her husband. The Lord knows our weaknesses and knew that Jenn needed clear confirmation, so that when the trials came, she would not be able to argue the calling. God could have given the "dream" to me but instead He gave it to the one who needed it most. He knew that she needed that personal touch. She needed to know that God was calling and directing her and therefore, would go before her. Neither one of us wanted to go, but this "lightning bolt" struck us into action. We were both perfectly content living our comfortable Christian lives. If we did not receive such a bold sign from the Lord, we could have easily passed this all by. However, knowing without a shadow of doubt that God wanted us to go, we had to quickly get over our wants and live like we have always claimed. We needed to really live for God. Thus begun the battle of dying to self and surrendering to God.

July 2, 2006

I'm so torn. I love my life, yet feel so distant from everything here. I feel sick to my stomach because I'm afraid. I don't want to give up everything here. Everything I've always wanted is here. I have friends and family I love. God, I'm broken. I don't know what to do. I'm so sad- You can't possibly want us to leave- to move across the country. We have a ministry here! I can't think of anything else. I just want to throw up. I want to forget that I ever heard from You last night.

July 28, 2006

Please continue to transform me. Please show us how and when to get to where we are going. Lord, prepare me and strengthen me. I have so many fears. Give me strength and keep Satan far from us. "May your glory rest in this place. May it go forth from here to the nations."

August 9, 2006

I do not want to go to Africa. Sometimes I think it would just be easier to stay- less conflict. A couple of people are being used by Satan to create fear in my life. The things people say. Lord help me to keep my eyes on You and what you are calling me to do daily. I want to be so in sync with You that I hear from You constantly. Empty me and fill me entirely with You. "Lord, I want more of You. Living water rain down on me. Lord I need more of You. Living breath of life come fill me up. I'm hungry for You."

As a pastor, there were multiple times that I was taught the importance of bringing all things to the elders of the church and allowing them to be the ones who send out. After much discussion, we decided that the next step we needed to take was to talk to the leadership at the church. If they were against it, then we would consider it a closed door at that time. In retrospect, though my intentions were good, I have realized that I alone am responsible for walking in obedience to the Lord. While it is important to listen and carefully consider what godly men have to share, the burden of faithfulness lies solely on the individual. My responsibility is to listen to God and follow His voice and not the voice of men.

"We speak as those approved by God to be entrusted with the gospel. We are not trying to please people but God, who tests our hearts." – 1 Thessalonians 2:4

In my heart, I did not think that this calling would be received well. I imagined that our senior pastor would say, "It sounds really neat, but I do not think this is the right time." Much to my surprise, he was very supportive and said that He believed that God was speaking to us and that we should continue to seek Him. And that is exactly what we did...

October 21, 2006

I've had another roller coaster week. (I was hoping that the elders would say that we were not to go to Africa. I was hoping that the Lord would show them otherwise. I really don't want to move to Africa, but I am also aware of the blatant direction the Lord is taking our family) After the elders decided last Sunday that the decision was in our hands, I felt afraid- we were really going to go. I was having anxiety all over again, just like in July. But you, oh God, are so good. You have sent encouragement. 1Thess 5:24 "he who calls you is faithful to do it." After 2 days of fretting, I felt a calmness from you –a peace. I felt like you were telling me "day by day". Why would I be freaking out about spending 5 years in Africa when you haven't told us we were going for 5 years? You have just called us to GO. It could be for 1 month, 16 months, or 26 months. We don't know, so why worry. I need to trust. You have always been so good. You know exactly what I need so in you I place my trust.

YOUR SEARCH...

Is there an area in your life that God has been leading you and you have been fighting it? Make a list of the reasons keeping you from acting on those decisions.

As you look at those reasons, consider their foundation. What makes them Biblical, God-honoring reasons or selfish, man-centered reasons?

Pray that God would give you the ability to clearly distinguish between man's wisdom and God's calling in your life.

"When he has brought out all his own, he goes on ahead of them, and his sheep follow him because they know his voice."
– John 10:4

CHAPTER FOUR

ARE YOU SURE?

One amazing night of revelation from God is wonderful, but could it be enough? Maybe there were subliminal messages in the movie. Maybe we had just eaten something the night before that had gone rancid! In our hearts we knew what God was asking us to do but our flesh needed more proof. We also needed more information. There was so much missing, like the when and the how.

Even figuring out where Mambia was located took some time. You see, Mambia is not one of the 47 countries that make up the continent of Africa. It's not even one of the well-known cities found in one of those countries. It is, in fact, a small, unknown village in a country that is also not familiar to most. As we searched for information about Mambia, we found it difficult to pinpoint the country that it was in. Finally, with the help of Google Earth, we determined that it was in the country of Guinea (not to be confused with Papua New Guinea, Equatorial Guinea or Guinea-Bissau!), which is a small country about the size of Oregon located in the west coast of the continent. The national language of Guinea is French and 85-

90% of the people are Muslim. This was not encouraging information for us. We did not speak French, had never been to Africa and had never ministered to Muslims!

Mambia is located between Conakry and Kindia

"We did not speak French, had never been to Africa and had never ministered to Muslims!"

Once again, God knew exactly what we needed to continue moving ahead. Over the next few months we were blown away by the confirmations that we received from the Lord. As we sought His direction, He clearly began to show us the way. In the beginning, we did not share what was going on except with our pastor, family, close friends, and the elders. As we did share though, the people we talked to also began to receive confirmations for us as well. Whenever we experienced or saw something that seemed out of the ordinary or miraculous, we wrote it down. Each of these events helped us become further convinced that we were hearing from the Lord...

1) The day after sharing the story with our senior pastor, he received an email from Calvary Chapel. The subject line said, "Calvary Chapels in Africa." The content of the email was an Excel spreadsheet listing all the fellowships in Africa. At first glance he thought the email was from me. He then realized that it was not and was very surprised since it was so random and something that he had never received before. He then forwarded the email to me. As I looked at it, I thought he had done some research for me. Then I noticed that he had just forwarded it. We were both very encouraged and felt that it was a small confirmation from the Lord.

2) A short while later, I shared with a good friend of mine named Lance. That night as we were heading to church, both of us were separately listening to the same message on the radio. The message was all about "going" and I sat in the parking lot a minute while the speaker drove the message home. It totally felt like he was speaking to me. As I got out and headed to the Junior High room, I ran into Lance. "Oh my gosh!" he said. "I just heard an amazing message that was all about what you guys are doing." He seemed just as

excited as I was to hear the Lord, once again, encourage and guide us.

3) My mom and my sister, Rebecca, came up to Bakersfield from the Los Angeles area for a short visit. I shared with the two of them what God had been showing to us and what we were planning on doing. My sister sat there and listened with a funny look on her face. As I finished, I asked her what was wrong. She said, "You are never going to believe this. Last night my friend and I were talking about visiting Africa someday. I stopped and told my friend that I could see my brother and his wife going to Africa to be missionaries someday."

4) After sharing the news with my dad he called some friends named Jeff and Martha who attended church with us, to tell them what we had shared. Jenn and I did not know it at the time, but they were former missionaries in Africa. When they heard what we were doing, they were very excited. They said that they had been praying for quite a while that someone at our church would get a heart for missions. We also found out that the country they served in bordered the country we were going to. Shortly after that, we met with them to look at pictures and hear about their time in Africa.

5) The day after meeting with Jeff and Martha, we "randomly" ended up sitting just a few seats away from them at a movie theater. If that wasn't enough, we then overheard the people directly behind us talking about how they had just gotten back from Africa. We turned around and talked with them for a while about their time there and shared a little about what we were doing.

6) The Children's Ministry Director at our church was in Israel and did not know what was going on. She emailed our senior pastor one day during her trip and told him that she felt like the Lord was doing something new in our fellowship. She was not sure what but felt that it was a good thing. When she returned from Israel, and we shared the news with her, she said that it all made sense with what she had been feeling.

7) Another neat thing that happened was how God had already been preparing us financially to go. About a year before we felt called to be missionaries, we had opened a vacation account at the bank. The goal was that we would go to Africa for a wildlife safari on our ten-year anniversary. We would be using that for Africa but just not in the way we had planned. God definitely has a sense of humor!

8) At the beginning of the year, the senior pastor at our church said that he wanted the theme of the year to be "Go". Because of that, we structured our Wednesday and Friday night Bible studies around the theme of missions and outreach. I also taught about what God was preparing me to do.

Someone might look at one or two situations I have just described as some sort of coincidence, but with so many taking place in such a short time, we were even more convinced that God was confirming His call on our lives.

Shortly after feeling called to Guinea, there were a few key moments where Jeremiah 1:4-8 was brought to me. It was a passage of encouragement as well as a calling upon my own life. Due to the impact it had on my life, we later decided to name the ministry after this passage. The name "One Jeremiah" is a bit of a play on words. It refers to Jeremiah Chapter One and also to the desire that we would also be someone, like Jeremiah was. It was our desire that we would be willing to go to the people and the places that God called us and that fear would not be an obstacle.

"The word of the Lord came to me, saying,
'Before I formed you in the womb I knew you, before you were born I set you apart; I appointed you as a prophet to the nations.'

'Alas, Sovereign Lord,' I said, 'I do not know how to speak; I am too young.'

But the Lord said to me, 'Do not say, 'I am too young.' You must go to everyone I send you to and say whatever I command you. Do not be afraid of them, for I am with you and will rescue you,' declares the Lord." – Jeremiah 1:4-8

YOUR SEARCH...

Do you have a "life verse" or a passage that means a lot to you? What is it and what does it mean to you?

When was the last time and situation where you saw confirmation of something God was doing in your life?

If there are any areas currently where you need confirmation, pray and ask God to clearly provide that additional direction and encouragement.

"Then the disciples went out and preached everywhere, and the Lord worked with them and confirmed his word by the signs that accompanied it." – Mark 16:20

CHAPTER FIVE
WE NEED MORE

All right, God! We got it. We are supposed to go to Guinea, West Africa...but that's only a small portion of the process. There are so many other details that still need answers. How do we get there? When do we go? What do we do when we get there?

These were the questions that we were really praying through as we neared the end of 2006. We became aware of a mission's conference in Murrieta Hot Springs that was put on by Calvary Chapel of Costa Mesa. Our church leadership blessed us by making that trip possible. There was such a strong feeling that we would receive a very large missing piece of the puzzle at that conference.

It was a great conference and it was exactly what we needed. We were so encouraged by the speakers and sessions and it gave us a renewed passion to do the will of God. We were amazed to listen to each speaker, as almost every one of them spoke about ministering to Muslims. Just before one of the main sessions, the host told us that someone very special had dropped in as he was passing through Murrieta. He asked the man to come up before the session speaker and share for five minutes on what God was doing in his life and ministry. His time was brief, but as he finished, he said, "And my grandson is now serving as a missionary in Guinea, West Africa". Jenn and I almost flew out of our seats. Guinea! What were the chances?!

I watched as the man left the stage and headed for the back door. I raced out of the auditorium, determined to catch him before he left. As I circled around the back, I caught him and his wife just as they were leaving. I introduced myself and asked them who his grandson was. He told me that his son's name was Jim and his wife was Becki. They were serving with the Christian and Missionary Alliance mission organization. This was a group that we were very familiar with. In fact, Jenn and I had actually graduated from a C&MA school in Northern California. I wrote their names down and, in my mind, hoped that one day we might be able to meet this family. Little did we know that we would not only eventually meet them, but they would also become friends of ours in Guinea!

Even with all the positive things that took place at the conference, there was still something missing by the end of the last day. We had not personally met anyone who was working or had worked in West Africa. We were told by some Calvary Chapel pastors we met that we would be blazing a new trail. Most of Calvary's work was taking place in English-speaking parts of Africa. Some might think it sounds exciting to be blazing a new trail. We did not! We like paved roads, maps and things that are NOT blazing! Our goal was to find a connection. We wanted someone to partner with. It would have been great to have someone who had been there before and could offer some advice, but it did not look like we were going to get any of those things.

"What some might call coincidence, I call answered prayer."

It was the last night of the conference and, although we were a little disappointed, we were still encouraged and grateful that we had gone. That night, after the last session of the conference, we stopped by the campus coffee shop to get some milk for the kids. Jenn was standing in line, and I was standing off to one side. A man walked up behind her to order coffee. She turned and casually greeted him. He introduced himself as John. Noticing a distinct accent, Jenn asked "May I ask where you are from." The man responded that he was from Mali, West Africa. Jenn was very excited. She quickly turned towards me and called me over. "This man is from West Africa," she exclaimed. I introduced myself and told him that we were feeling called to go to Guinea, West Africa. His face immediately lit up. "I have a friend named Pius, who is a pastor in Guinea. He would love to meet you!" I told him that we were planning on starting out in the capital city of Conakry but that we had no connections with anyone there. He informed us that his friend was actually pastoring a church in Conakry. "This is a God-thing," he said. He had taken the words right out of my mouth! What some might call coincidence, I call answered prayer. Because it was late and the children were tired, we agreed to meet for breakfast the next morning to talk more.

We were so excited and anxious that we could hardly wait until morning. This "chance" meeting was exactly what we were hoping for with this conference. It did not take long however, for us to start doubting God's plan. I began to ask myself, "What if this man doesn't show up for breakfast?" Our one and only connection would be gone and we would be back to square one. How faithless we can be sometimes! God is always in control. When breakfast came the next morning, we picked a table in the front of the large dining hall and saved spots for this man and his family. Other friends walked in the dining room and wanted to sit with us, but we told them that we were saving a few spots. After what seemed like forever, we were excited and relieved to see John walk through the dining hall doors. At breakfast, he explained how perfect God's timing was. He was originally planning to see Pius before the conference, but it did not work out so now his plan was to see Pius after this conference. They would be meeting in Mali. John told us that we should call him in one week and he would be in Africa. At that point, he would be put us on the phone with Pastor Pius. "Here is my phone number. Call me in one week and I will put you on the phone with my friend." Jenn and I were blown away. It sounded a little weird and perhaps too good to be true! What an amazing thing that God did by divinely arranging this meeting. It was also just like his character to wait until the very last minute! He had given us exactly what we needed and so much more.

YOUR SEARCH...

It is important to put yourself in a place where God can speak to you and do the miraculous. When was the last time you listened to a message or sat through a sermon and really prayed that God would show you something new? What was the result?

What distractions might keep you from growing in the Lord or seeing the Holy Spirit move and work in your life?

Do a search for a conference or event that might challenge you and your faith and make a wholehearted effort to attend.

"I will instruct you and teach you in the way you should go; I will counsel you and watch over you." – Psalm 32:8

CHAPTER SIX

THE TEST

Often a moment of encouragement and confirmation is followed by a trial or test of faith. This would be the case for us as we left the missions conference in Murrieta and our divine appointment with Pastor John.

When we got back to Bakersfield, we shared the good news with our pastor. We discussed the next option and decided that it was a good time to tell the church body. On Sunday, January 14th, 2007, I shared this new development in our lives with the congregation. It was a very difficult thing to do. People were shocked, especially since we seemed like such unlikely candidates. I do not think the majority of people we knew saw this coming. We had been serving this body for over eight years now and developed some very strong relationships. To say that we were sad about leaving would be a huge understatement. Leaving the youth and the ministry we had there was one of the most emotional things I have ever had to do. I believe this is often an indicator that God might be leading you in a new direction. When every day is a struggle, it is easy to think that God wants you to go elsewhere. When you love what you do and you feel called to something new, there is a good chance that God is behind it because it goes against what your flesh desires.

During one of our Sunday services, I was given time to share with the congregation, what our plans for the future were. If you are interested in hearing this message, we have uploaded the audio to the link below...

https://youtu.be/mxveSpBndns

During our time at the mission's conference, I felt like the Lord was showing me that it would be a good thing to visit Guinea before moving there. This visit was not meant to be a "test" because I already knew what we were being called to do. Instead, I would approach it like the spies who were sent into Canaan to observe the land in Numbers 13. God had already given them the land, but they were going to explore and bring back a report. I was very excited to go. Jenn did not want to go because she had heard that the poor living conditions in the country were more than she had ever experienced. Seeing it beforehand would just make it that much harder to actually move there. After discussing this potential trip with the staff, the senior pastor said he would make the journey with me. Jenn was very relieved that he was willing to accompany me on the trip.

"Every step of the way, it became more obvious that God would continue to clear our path."

About two weeks later, I purchased tickets for our pastor and myself to visit at the end of March. We were excited to go and began getting our shots needed for the trip, as well as our visas. One of the things that continues to amaze me, was how the Lord had orchestrated our connection with Pastor Pius in Conakry. As we began to apply for visas, I discovered that Guinea did not issue tourist visas. To enter the country we needed to have a letter of invitation from someone already in the country. Praise the Lord that we had met this man John in Southern California at the conference. God knew we needed this connection and that without it, we probably would not have been given a visa. Every step of the way, it became more obvious that God would continue to clear our path.

As we continued preparations for the trip, it felt good to be moving forward. Although we were not excited about moving to Guinea, we were comforted knowing that at least they had been a stable country. There was not much about the country's problems in the news like some other African countries. Well, all that soon changed for us.

Days after purchasing the tickets I received an email from our new friend in Guinea, Pius. In the email he said not to worry about what the news was saying regarding the things going on in Guinea. "What's going on in Guinea?" I thought. I began to look at some websites which report news in that part of the world. Sure enough, the country was beginning to experience some political troubles. Up until that point, everything I read said that Guinea was a fairly stable country.

Now, they were reporting protests and fighting in the streets. Things quickly deteriorated from there. A few days later, I read that the President had declared marshal law. Military were controlling the streets. People were only allowed out of their homes for a few hours each day. During that time, over 150 people were killed in the protests, most of them by the country's military.

Now, right after I had just purchased tickets, all flights had been canceled in and out of the country. Most of the missionaries living in the country had been evacuated. I was counseled to get my money back and postpone the trip. I did not know what I could do at this point. It was completely out of my hands. Even if I decided to proceed with the trip in March, there were no flights available and I highly doubted that they would issue me a visa. I began to pray asking the Lord to show us what He wanted us to do.

February 7, 2007

Paul and our pastor had purchased plane tickets to Guinea but with the unrest in Guinea we were not sure whether or not to pursue sinking money into this trip (vaccinations, visas, etc) and whether they could even get into the country.

We felt very discouraged during this time. Here we were taking this step of faith to move to a third world country and then the doors get shut. We seriously could not get into the country at this time. We began to pray and ask the Lord what He wanted us to do. Did we hear him right when He said to go to Guinea? Was this the end of the road for now? This is something that we have continued to see over and over in our lives. Shortly after we take a step in faith, we are met with a difficult challenge or obstacle. As Christians, I think it is important for us to recognize the difference between a closed door and an obstacle to overcome. One of the ways to distinguish the difference is to pray. God promises that He will guide us if we seek Him.

"You will seek me and find me when you seek me with all your heart." – Jeremiah 29:13

For a Valentine's present, I gave Jenn a weekend to go out of town by herself. On February 23rd, 2007, while Jenn was away, God woke me up very early in the morning. I spent that opportunity praying about the trip I was supposed to take in March and about our family moving to Guinea. I specifically asked God to show me what I should do. As I prayed, I strongly felt that God was reminding me that he had not shown me anything different yet and that I should continue moving forward. With this new sense of peace and encouragement from the Lord, I began to pray that God would also give clear direction to Jenn regarding my plans to visit Guinea in March. Later that morning when Jenn got up, I received a call from her. She was spending time with the Lord and said that she felt God telling her that I should continue moving ahead with this March trip. I was so amazed how God had spoken the same thing to both of us within hours of each other, yet miles away!

February 23, 2007

I've been confused lately with all the riots and violence in Guinea. I confess that I was angry. I felt like it was hard enough for me to decide to move to Africa, but at least Guinea was stable- now this. Over 100 people have been killed. Only a few missionaries are even there. I'm in unrest again. No flights can enter Guinea right now so Paul and I are praying for your wisdom and guidance. It says in your word to pray and you will receive. Paul and I have been praying for guidance and wisdom and peace for weeks. Should Paul cancel their plane tickets now? What to do?

Well, you are amazing. As I was spending time with you this morning I felt like you were saying "I haven't told you not to go-have faith." I was directed to the scripture through a Bible study on faith at the time (how convenient) Hebrews 11:8 "By faith, Abraham, when called to go to a place he would later receive as his inheritance, obeyed and went, even though he did not know where he was going." Have faith. Who cares if airplanes are not flying right now, you allowed these tickets to be purchased for a reason. We need to have faith. You can open up flights the day before. You are God and you can do anything.

I'm in Valencia right now. I was excited to call Paul this morning and share with him what I felt like the Lord was showing me. When I called him to tell him that we need to keep moving forward and trust God, he said the Lord had showed him the same thing and was praying at 4 am that He would show me the same thing too. Wow! Our God is incredible.

I emailed our pastor who was aware of the current situation. I told him that I would completely understand if he was not comfortable going but that I was still planning on making the trip. Knowing that our first stopover was in France, I told him that I would go as far as the plane would take me and then let God do the rest. He emailed me back the next day and said that he would make the trip as well and that he was looking forward to the adventure.

Just a few days after this I checked back online to see how things were going in Guinea. I was amazed to see the new reports. Peace had been restored. People were happy with some new decisions that had been made. Everyone was out and about shopping again. Even the airlines had begun making flights back into the country. One website actually called it a miracle! Jenn and I believe that this was a test to see if we would turn back when there was trouble. We have since apologized to our friends in Guinea for the problems that our lack of faith caused in their country ;)

Just before our trip in March, God provided yet another divine appointment. A missionary in Guinea, named J.D., happened to be in California on furlough at the time. Even more "coincidental," was the fact he had just spoken at my grandmother's church in Northern California. My grandmother forwarded his information to us and we quickly contacted him. By God's grace, we were able to meet him in Long Beach during which time he gave us so much helpful information. He was excited about the possibility of more missionaries working Guinea.

March 1, 2007

Very cool. Drove down to Long Beach today to meet with JD. Paul found him from the internet after his granny had sent us his newsletters mentioning that he was home for furlough. Just so happens he was coming through California for some speaking engagements and we were able to meet with him. It was a divine appointment. We learned so much from him. It was a great visit.

March 18, 2007

I am very emotional today. I'm broken but I know that it's a good place to be. I'm emotional because our God is so amazing. I'm humbled that He would choose me to go. I'm afraid because I'm not qualified. I'm nervous about needing so much strength. I'm apprehensive about persecution. I'm guilty of being too comfortable here. I'm selfish, I'm scared, I'm honored, I'm excited, I'm sad, I'm afraid of loneliness. I don't want to give up my friends or my family. But yet... your works are wonderfully manifold. My God you are so good. Your ways are higher than mine. Your love endures forever. You give and you take away but blessed be the Lord. My lips will praise you. You give strength to the weary. I am persecuted but not crushed. To Him be the glory forever and ever amen.

As the trip approached, the idea of moving became even more real. Talking about moving to another country and actually going there are two very different things. Although the path was being clearly laid out, I had no idea how I would handle spending time in such an unfamiliar environment.

YOUR SEARCH...

When was the last time your faith was challenged or your obedience tested?

How did you handle that situation and is there anything you would do differently if given the chance?

Ask God to give you strength to overcome any fears or obstacles you are currently facing.

"I have told you these things, so that in me you may have peace. In this world you will have trouble. But take heart! I have overcome the world." – John 16:33

CHAPTER SEVEN
THE TRIP

I had never been to Africa. My only trips out of the country were to Mexico and to Scotland. In college, I had spent a month in Scotland. It was an amazing trip but not terribly difficult. I slept in nice beds, ate great food (minus the blood pudding) and did not need a translator...except for a few times in northern Scotland. I think they were speaking English, but it was often hard to tell! My time in Mexico was short and I already knew some Spanish. It was there, though, that I first got a glimpse of some real-life poverty. However, neither of those trips prepared me for what I would experience in Africa.

As I was sitting in the airport in France waiting to board a flight for Guinea, I became overwhelmed at the weight of what I was doing. Everyone waiting for the flight was speaking a different language. I think it was French but I could not understand one word of it. Most of the people were African and were wearing unique African clothing. It was the afternoon and it hit me that we would be landing late at night, in a country we had never been to, with people who we could not understand and with no one there to even guide us. What was I thinking? How in the world was this supposed to work?! The adventurous type might find some strange excitement at a moment like this, but not me. I suddenly wished I had a hole I could crawl into.

"This place was not only unfamiliar, it was scary and intimidating."

When the plane landed, and we walked out onto the runway, all my fears were confirmed. This place was not only unfamiliar, it was scary and intimidating. We entered the terminal and people began pushing past us to get through the security checkpoint. I held tightly to my passport and moved to the window. Somehow, we managed to smile and nod as our passports were looked over and eventually stamped for approval. Once through this checkpoint, we entered the baggage claim area. Immediately, we were bombarded by men who wanted to collect our luggage for us. Thankfully one of them spoke some broken English, so we followed him towards the unloading belt. When we had retrieved our bags, we headed outside.

Things outside were even more shocking to the system. There was trash everywhere. Many of the locals sat around in the dark, smoking cigarettes. As a mostly sheltered Californian, I felt like a parakeet being sized up by a group of hungry cats. When we reached the parking lot, we were escorted to a van that we were told to get into, so that we could be driven to the hotel. Having done some research on the dangers of foreigners being overcharged, I asked him how much it would cost. He said not to worry about it and just get in. Being the frugal person I am, I was determined not to get into the van until I knew what we would be charged. I tried again to get an answer, meanwhile, my mind began imagining a ride in this van that would end at a dark alley with theft and perhaps murder. The man ignored the question again and reached for our bags. Suddenly, I heard my name being called. I turned around to see three men, one of whom was Pastor Pius. I breathed a huge sigh of relief and quickly rushed to their side. What a blessing it was to be rescued by these guys! They took us to their car and we headed towards the hotel while the man who had helped us get our luggage chased after us demanding money.

As we drove along the streets of Conakry in the middle of the night, I was in shock. At first, I figured that the airport was in a bad part of town and things were going to start improving around the next corner. Well, the improved next corner never came. Each street was filled with crowds of people, piles of trash and random fires. To my inexperienced nostrils, the smells were almost unbearable. The entire city looked like a war zone. I tried my best to hold it together and engage in some sort of conversation with our hosts. We finally arrived at the hotel and checked into our room. From what I could tell online, this was one of the best hotels in the city. It was definitely not up to the standards of American hotels but it was great to have a place to lie down finally.

When I put my head on the pillow, I lost it. I began to weep. My heart ached, like I just lost a loved one. How can I bring my family to a place like this? I said to myself. "I don't want to do this, Lord" I cried. Why would you send us here? In the middle of my anguish, it was obvious that something needed to happen for this move to take place. At this point. I would not be able to return to America with a good report. I could picture myself in front of the congregation saying, "There are giants in the land and I am not going!" It would take the work of God to change my heart.

We spent the next day with our new friends. They showed us around the city. It was a little less frightening in the day but now my fears had faces. From the perspective of this foreigner, there were little to no redeeming qualities to be found. Here is an email that I sent to Jenn during that trip...

> *The city (Conakry) is very dirty and noisy. When the traffic is not bumper to bumper (literally!), the cars fly around like NASCAR drivers-weaving in and out of everyone. There are no lights, signals or street signs. You either force your way in or you are stuck forever. Pedestrians do not have the right of way here. They dodge cars like little animals trying to avoid becoming roadkill. There is non-stop honking of horns. People line every street. Some are there to sell things like vendors on the streets of Mexico. Others are there to beg from the passing cars. Who knows what the other million are doing? Everyone just hangs out.*

Driving down the streets, you can look down alleyways and see sights like you might see on a Red Cross or World Vision commercial. Tiny little shack "houses" all grouped tightly together. They are made of decaying wood strips or rusted out metal. I can't imagine how they must get pounded when the rains come. Kids sit in the dirt or mud as women clean laundry in the streets. The smells can be nauseating. There are animals here as well. Cats, dogs, goats, frogs, lizards, ducks, cows, a couple parrots, one monkey and thousands of bats at dusk!

This is all so different from the Africa I had always imagined. As you move away from the city, you can begin to see some of the beauty that is sometimes thought of in relation to Africa. There are hills and trees and beautiful rivers. Everything is green and lush. Even away from the city though, you do not escape the poverty. Kids in the countryside still stand on the road with various items for sale. They "repair" potholes in the road and as cars come, they try to stop them with vines and ask for money for their "services". It is a very different place where waves of excitement cover the subtle fear of a lonely outsider.

YOUR SEARCH...

What is the scariest place you have ever been in and why?

Have you ever felt the presence of God during a time of fear? What was it like?

Thank God for His protection and guidance through difficult circumstances in your life.

"Though I walk in the midst of trouble, you preserve my life. You stretch out your hand against the anger of my foes; with your right hand you save me." – Psalm 138:7

CHAPTER EIGHT
IT EXISTS!

As we spent time with our new friends in Guinea, I explained to them why we were here and about the vision that my wife had. Suddenly, their demeanor changed. "Then we need to go to Mambia," they said. To them, it seemed pointless to wander around the capital city when God had given us the name of a specific village. I agreed and was very excited to actually see the place we had, literally, only dreamed of!

"Great! So you know Mambia then?" "No" was the reply. "We've never heard of it. But we will ask around."

It was not exactly what I was hoping to hear. I realized that we were being called to an obscure location, but it would be nice if at least the people living in the same country had heard of it! The next day when they returned to pick us up from our hotel, they informed us that they had located Mambia and that it was on a paved road only 50 miles (ca. 80 km) from where we were. I had never considered that it could have been much further or that we might not have been able to get there by car. We were so blessed that it was located where it was.

Despite the short distance, this was not a short, easy trip. We sat squished together in the back seat of a small car for a very bumpy two-hour ride. We hung our heads out the car windows in an effort to have some fresh air. Instead, we were met with the fumes from massive, overloaded trucks and minivans packed with more than 30 passengers that raced by. Although their laws were unfamiliar to me, I was pretty sure there were no smog laws, at least none that were being enforced! Along the drive we were stopped at three checkpoints. Though we passed through two of them without any issues, the police at one checkpoint refused to let us pass until our driver paid him some money. Apparently this is common when they see foreigners in a car and assume they can benefit from the situation.

Once we made it past the checkpoints, it was not long before we came upon a sign with the word "Mambia." It was an exhilarating feeling to see this word that we had talked about and researched for so long. The main portion of the village was a cluster of buildings and huts alongside the main road. If we were driving fast and blinked, we might have missed it. Soon we had parked, and we began to ask around in order to locate the chief. After he was located, we were ushered into a small, grass-roof hut just off the road. By this time, we were beginning to draw a crowd and many women and children surrounded the hut, sticking their heads in the openings to get a glimpse of the foreigners.

"Even here, in the middle of this insignificant village, He was using complete strangers to strengthen His call on our lives!"

As we prepared to tell them why we were there, our local friends quickly realized that none of the men in the hut could speak French. They only spoke the local language, which is Susu. Our friends did not know Susu and therefore it was necessary to find someone who could speak both Susu and French. After a few minutes of looking around awkwardly at each other, a boy of about 13 or 14 years was brought into the hut. Because he was one of the children who actually attended school, he was able to speak some French, as well as Susu. It was quite an experience as the pastor spoke in English to one of his friends who then spoke French to the young boy who then translated that into Susu for the chief! When we explained that our plan was for my family to return in June and live there, the place broke out in cheers and applause. They said to us "Our home is your home." This welcome was exactly what I needed. The fears were not gone, but I was encouraged. God had reconfirmed His calling for my family. It was an incredible reminder of His omnipresence. Even here, in the middle of this insignificant village, He was using complete strangers to strengthen His call on our lives!

After more pleasantries, we asked the chief what the greatest need in his village was. Without hesitation, he replied,

"Water!" It was so humbling to hear this answer. If I were asked the same question, I am not sure what my response would have been. Did I even have any REAL physical needs? Wasn't the whole world in my grasp? Here in this village though, water is the source of life. They spend many hours collecting it. The quality of the water they find, could ultimately mean the difference between life and death. From that moment, I made it a goal that we would do whatever we could to provide the village with clean water.

Local woman collecting water from a stagnant river

March 22, 2007

   Today Paul found Mambia. AMAZING! I can't believe it exists; something I saw in a dream. Amazingly cool how God works.

YOUR SEARCH...

   Do you have a dream or a desire that has not yet been fulfilled? What is it?

   How would or could God be honored or glorified if this came to pass?

   Ask God to work in you so that your desires and dreams match His heart and plan.

   "Many are the plans in a person's heart but it is the Lord's purpose that prevails." – Proverbs 19:21

CHAPTER NINE
FINAL PREPARATIONS

One of the issues that has come up over and over again is the issue of proper training and preparation. How does one prepare for life as a missionary in a foreign country? What are the requirements before you leave? I had returned from my "scouting" trip to Guinea and now these questions began to surface more and more.

Our plan was to leave in the summer, but we still had no formal training. I had spent one month in Scotland and both of us had spent a week in Mexico. That was our extent of mission's training. What about the language barrier? When we had discovered that the national language was French, we began learning little bits at a time. Six months later though, and we still only knew some basic greetings. Even French, though, was not enough in Mambia. As I had seen on our trip, most of the people in the village only spoke Susu. Since the Susu Language Center in Bakersfield had recently closed, we did not see many opportunities to pursue that. I am joking, of course. You would be hard-pressed to find even one person in California that speaks Susu!

Another part of the preparation process for many, is financial support. How much money will you need and who will provide it? During our March trip, one of my goals was to determine, as best as possible, what the cost would be for my family to live in Guinea. We shopped in grocery stores, checked housing prices and took notes on all that we found. From what we could see, the cost for food would probably be about the same as we were paying in the states. It looked like we could get a somewhat decent place to live for about $500 a month. On returning home, I proposed that our living expenses would be between $1200 and $1500 a month. For us though, the finances were never a big concern. From early on, our pastor let us know that the church would take care of our financial needs. Though we did not know all the details, it was great to know that our church was behind us. It was truly a blessing that we did not have to worry about support and it took a huge weight off of our shoulders. We knew that there were many struggles ahead but, thankfully, finances would not be one of them.

"There were so many unanswered questions, but we knew that they would be answered as we continued to take steps of faith in obedience."

So what was next? Did we have enough to sell everything and move to a foreign country to share the gospel with Muslims in a language that we did not know? Some said we needed more. They encouraged us to hook up with an organization or a group that was already working over there. We prayed through this and began looking for doors that God might show us. Over the next few months, I sent many emails and made many phones calls to various pastors, missionaries and organizations, in an attempt to come alongside an established work in Guinea. One possibility for us was New Tribes Missions. Early on, when we began researching Guinea, we found that they had a strong presence in the country. On their website they had lots of personnel needs in Guinea. One in particular jumped out at us. It was the position of a Guesthouse Director. We thought it would be a great way to support the missionaries that were already living and working in the country. It would also give us time to learn the language a little better. I contacted them in March to discuss what the job entailed and to see if it might be something that God was leading us to do. What I found out is that they had recently been kicked out of their guesthouse and currently were attempting to relocate. Because there was now, no longer a need for that position, that door was quickly closed.

A second possibility came at the mission's conference in Southern California. There we met the guys from Saving Grace World Missions. They worked at a small Calvary Chapel in Yorba Linda, CA and were involved in training and sending missionaries all over the world. They had nothing going on in West Africa but encouraged us to contact them. After returning from Guinea in March, I decided to follow up on that lead. We contacted the church and received an application packet by email. Within a few weeks we finished the application and sent it off. In the meantime, though we did not have all the details, we knew that we were called to go, so we bought our tickets to Guinea departing in June. However, not knowing how long we were going to be there, we bought four one-way tickets. There were so many unanswered questions, but we knew that they would be answered as we continued to take steps of faith in obedience.

It was almost three months before we finally received an email from Saving Grace World Missions. I had already written that off as a closed door. Come to find out, they had misplaced our application and it was sitting in a pile of other paperwork unnoticed. Although our departure was only scheduled for about a month away, they felt that they might be able to help us by handling the financial portion of the ministry. We had no clue how we were going to receive money at that point and were very grateful that they contacted us. We drove down in the beginning of June to spend some time with my mom and also to meet with the guys at Saving Grace. The meeting went very well. They wished we had more time to do training but said that they would gladly partner with us. This was a huge blessing and something that they continued to do up until we received our non-profit status years later.

Looking back on all that took place before we left, I really believe there was a reason that God wanted us to go in the "unprepared" status that He had called us. I am reminded of Acts 4:13 where the crowd listening to Peter and John saw that they were untrained and realized that they must have been with Jesus. Much of what God did through us while in Guinea was in spite of anything that we had known or learned. Often, other missionaries in the country would share how shocked they were at the amazing things God was doing. It was apparent that we had nothing to offer, but somehow God was working through weak vessels. The following is one of my journal entries after we had been living in Guinea for about two months.

PAUL'S JOURNAL

August 26, 2007

Some thoughts on preparation and training: I realized recently that so many times, these ideas of being prepared for the mission field are really clever disguises for fear. We do not want to go into a situation where we do not have control over our surroundings, so we do as much training as possible to make it a smooth transition. Have we forgotten that it is upon the rough seas we will see and experience miracles and see the face of God? Have we forgotten that we are already equipped to handle anything that comes at us? I can do ALL things through Christ? Not through proper training, but through surrender and reliance upon the Holy

Spirit. I can have years of language learning and cultural acquisition and still fail miserably because without Him I am nothing and my efforts are in vain. I can walk up to a man, have a complete understanding of his language, share the gospel in a culturally specific way, and use an eloquent three-point message, but the seed will wither and perish if God has not prepared the ground to receive it. Another man with no knowledge of a particular language and in an element where he has never been, can do a short object lesson and have the recipient on his knees in repentance because the man was led by the Holy Spirit. This is how God chooses to work because it is then that He alone gets the glory. He does not want to share the glory with the time and effort that you have put into preparing. After all, He could use a donkey to share His message if He wanted to. He used a small boy with very little battle experience to bring down the fiercest of competitors. David was prepared because he had been busy with the work of God for so long. He had been walking in obedience to the Lord for so long that it did not matter the size of the task, the result would always be that God would triumph. Ephesians 6:13-20 tells us that we are prepared when we are fitted with Christ. Everything we need, to battle against the enemy in any land and in any circumstance, we have when we put on Christ. He invented the tongues. He divided the cultures. He fashioned every land. Is there *anything too difficult for Him? Let Him be the victor!*

It is important for me to point out that I am not against missionary training, raising financial support and language learning. My point is that we often rely on these things or see them as necessary to complete God's calling on someone's life. There is a plaque that hangs in the Christian and Missionary Alliance guesthouse in Guinea that captures this concept. It says, "God does not call the qualified, He qualifies the called." I could not agree with that statement more. There were definitely gifts and talents that we had but our lack of competence made us completely reliant on God for the victory. Our story is not a formula of how it should be done, but rather a reminder that we each must pursue God's leading in our life and not follow the principles and qualifications laid out by man.

YOUR SEARCH...
What adventures have you spent time preparing for in life?

How have those preparations helped or, perhaps, hindered you?

What ministries do you have a desire to be involved in, but feel unqualified for?

Remind yourself today that God does not always call those who are the most prepared or equipped, but rather those who are available and ready to be used by Him.

"He chose the lowly things of this world and the despised things, and the things that are not, to nullify the things that are, so that no one may boast before him." – 1 Corinthians 1:28-29

CHAPTER TEN

THE ADVENTURE BEGINS

When we left America, we felt completely helpless and incapable of doing any kind of ministry for the Lord. It was definitely a leap of faith into a brand new and unknown world. I think this is exactly how God wanted it. He needed to reduce us to nothing so that His great power could be revealed in us.

JENN'S JOURNAL

June 13, 2007

"It's D-day (the day we move to Africa). I'm totally surprised and shocked at how emotionally stable I am. As I pondered why this was I realized that it's all the prayers and God's strength. It's AMAZING! I was thinking back to last year when this all started and how I cried so much then thinking about this upcoming day- and now here it is and I'm okay. I realized that God gives me strength for TODAY. Last year He wasn't giving

me strength for this day to come, He was giving me strength for THAT day."

June 13th came. It was the big moving day. We had been very nervous about this day for a long time. We wondered if we could really do it and, as we drove away, we learned another valuable lesson from the Lord; His strength sustains us in time of need. His grace is sufficient and His mercies are new every morning. God gives us what we need for that moment. Not usually for days in advance or for upcoming trials, but for that day. Just like the Lord provided daily for the Israelites in the wilderness, He always provides us daily with His strength and His comfort. We had never experienced it quite like before. A trial so anticipated, yet when the time came His peace covered us.

It's one of those situations that most have experienced, where your mind drifts into a snare of thinking, What if something like that happened to me? What if my kids or my husband died? What if....? This thought process is not from the Lord. If that trial should ever come, our God would hide us in the shadow of His wings. He covers us. He gives us peace that passes everyone else's understanding. Only those who have experienced His covering in time of need, grasp this concept. He is our shield. Though we might walk through the valley of the shadow of death, we will fear no evil. Instead, we will sing in the shadow of God's wings knowing that He is our Lord.

"God always loves to wait until the last minute!"

As we made the final preparations to leave, we got a real big picture that the enemy was trying to distract us from our mission. One of those areas of distraction was with regard to my passport. My passport was set to expire in about a year from our departure date. Since we were unsure of how long we would be in Guinea, I had sent it off to be renewed. Unfortunately, things got backed up and passports were taking much longer than they were supposed to. We were quite apprehensive as we headed down to Los Angeles to spend our last week with my mom. I still did not have my passport back and things were not looking good. They had put a rush on it, but we did not think it would make it in time. Finally, we got word that it would arrive...the day our flight was leaving! Talk about cutting it close! Not only that, another problem was that it had been sent to Bakersfield. I was able to arrange with a good friend of mine, Stephen, to bring the passport down for us. Thankfully it worked out beautifully, and we were able to have lunch with him and his girlfriend Ruth just before our plane left. As we have already seen, God always loves to wait until the last minute.

Another distraction came as we pulled up to Los Angeles International Airport. Tons of people had been sent out of one of the terminals and there were police everywhere. We quickly realized that it was our terminal. Upon going inside we discovered that there had been a bomb scare and all the people had just been evacuated. Thankfully, they opened the terminal back up just as we were walking in. As you can imagine, it was still a bit chaotic as people now crowded lines rushing to get their flights. At the ticket counter, I gave all of our information to the airline representative. After looking over the information, she asked me to wait for a few moments as she went over to talk to her manager.

Again I felt like we were in a spiritual battle. Not knowing exactly what was going on, I began praying right there at the counter that God's will would be done and that He would open doors for us. Aware of the situation, Jenn and the kids stood back and began praying as well. When the lady returned a few moments later, she told us that we were not booked on the flight. They did not have us listed as passengers anywhere! Before we could say much more than "WHAT?" her manager walked back over and said, "Put them on the flight" and then walked away! It was amazing. The same thing happened again when we got to the flight gate. This time we were paged to the front and told that we were not going to be able to get on. I explained that this was taken care of downstairs. He told us to wait again. Before walking away, he glanced at my carry on and said that my bag was too big and would not be allowed on the flight anyway. Once again, we stood there for a few minutes praying that God would take care of the situation. When he returned, he just waved us to the front of the line and on we went without checking our baggage and without another word about our tickets! We definitely saw the power of God that day.

After arriving in France and spending a few days sightseeing, we went to our connecting flight which was to stop in Senegal before continuing on to Guinea. Once again we arrived at the airport and went to check in. This time the woman explained that our flight had been canceled. They had tried to contact us but had no way to get a hold of us. As I attempted to figure out what the next step was, police suddenly began clearing out the whole terminal. There was another bomb scare here! The lady told me to come back when the terminal was open. I returned later to determine what to do. It was getting late and we were all tired and hungry. The attendant told me that our flight would leave the next day. She handed me some coupons and said, "These are for your meals. We have put you up in a hotel. You may take the free shuttle out front." We were so blessed! The hotel was beautiful and the food was incredible. It was such a wonderful gift of God's grace before our final departure. It definitely seemed that there was a battle going on in heavenly realms that day. How awesome to know that we are on the winning side when we put our hope in God!

June 25, 2007

Yesterday was Selah's birthday. It was emotionally rough. She asked several times about her friends coming and having a party. I really wanted to go home. I couldn't stop crying last night. I hate this and the sacrifice it is on my kids. It is hard. Today is better. We walked around Paris and got errands done because we fly out to Africa tomorrow. I'm nervous because if I hate being in Paris, how much more will I hate Africa?

YOUR SEARCH...

What are some recent discouragements you have faced in your life?

How can you tell the difference between God closing a door and Satan trying to discourage you?

Pray that God gives you strength to persevere through trials when walking in obedience to Him and that He gives you humility to change your actions when you are walking in the flesh.

"Ask and it will be given to you; seek and you will find; knock and the door will be opened to you. For everyone who asks receives; he who seeks finds; and to him who knocks, the door will be opened." – Matthew 7:7-8

CHAPTER ELEVEN
THE ARRIVAL

Despite the obvious victories, our battles were by no means over. Upon our arrival at the airport in Guinea, we discovered that only one of our four bags had arrived. Even worse than that, was the fact that mine was the only one which had come, meaning that Jenn and the kids had no clothes and there were no diapers for Cedar. This presented a big problem for us, especially since kids don't wear diapers in Guinea. We weren't ready to have our child urinating and defecating on the side of the road! Where were we going to find diapers? They next day I went back down to the airport to see if our things had arrived. They had not, but we were told that they would be there later that afternoon. God provided a very nice man who spoke English and said he would call when the things came in. Sure enough, he called back a short time later and when I arrived at the airport, he was out front with all our stuff on a cart.

For our first two nights in Guinea, we decided to stay at the plush and fancy Novotel hotel. I say that somewhat sarcastically. By Guinea standards, it was one of the nicest hotels they had at the time, but by American standards, it made a Best Western look like the Ritz. The carpets were stained and dirty. There was no evidence that the towels and sheets were changed regularly. The elevator would stop randomly due to the unpredictable electricity and the air conditioner did not operate for the entire time we were there. Despite its inconveniences however, it was a welcome harbor for Jenn and the kids. During the first two days, they hung out in the room and at the pool. For Jenn, it seemed like she had woken up from a bad dream. She was able to briefly put the reality of moving to a third world country out of her mind, as we remained somewhat secluded from the rest of Guinea during our stay at the hotel.

June 28, 2007

Oh my goodness! When we arrived in Guinea at 9 pm, we walked into a non-air conditioned building to fill out custom's paperwork and get our baggage. The kids had fallen asleep on the plane, so they were losing it while we stood in the building. Both kids were crying and I had sweat pouring down my back. We waited an hour for our bags but only got Paul's. All of a sudden, yelling started. The airport security told everyone that they were finished with baggage. The people were upset. I was too. I had nothing for me or the kids. I only had one diaper left. I couldn't understand how Paul got his bag, but we had none of the others. At 11 PM, we walked out into the twilight zone. Praise the Lord, Pius, Solomon and Joseph were there because our hotel shuttle had left since it was so late. The three men helped us get to the car. While we walked to the car, we were accompanied by the most beautiful African singing and drums. It was like our own personal parade. It was hilarious! As we drove to the hotel, I could not have imagined what I saw. It was so much worse than I thought. So much more extreme than television could capture. It was 11 PM and there were millions of people out, just sitting there. There were hundreds of campfires, houses that looked like they had been blown up during a war, and the smells were awful. It was the craziest thing I've ever seen. I could not believe my eyes. How can people live like this and how can this be so? Americans have so much, and yet they are living like this in Africa? Then we arrived at the "fanciest hotel" here. It looks like the worst Motel 6 I've ever seen, but it's a room. I showered with hotel shampoo, washed my face with the same stuff, and wore Paul's clothes to bed. Hopefully and prayerfully our bags will be here when the airport opens at 9 AM.

Two days later, we went to the C&MA guesthouse where we were scheduled to spend a week while we prepared to move into our house. Our time at the guesthouse proved to be the best thing for us. It was there that we met many of the missionaries working in Guinea. We made friends who were a comfort and an encouragement to us. We met other friends who went out of their way to help us and welcome us. We met people who would later become close friends. We met people who would inspire and challenge us. It seemed that many people had already heard about us. J.D. had emailed his friend Phil who had in turn emailed and talked to others about us. The word quickly spread and it was very interesting to us to see the reaction of the missionaries. All of them seemed amazed that we would come in the way that we did. Some of them were inspired by what they saw as a step of faith. Others were apprehensive about what they saw as a lack of planning and preparation. All in all though, the missionary community in Guinea quickly became our family away from home.

During our time at the Christian and Missionary Alliance guesthouse, we made some great connections and wonderful friends. A very nice couple from Canada went way out of their way to teach us the ropes and show us around. They also invited us over for lunch and took us shopping for some necessities.

We remained at the guesthouse for a few weeks as we got our house ready to move into. Communication was extremely challenging as we did not have phones for the first few weeks. We encouraged our friends and family to contact us through Skype once we did have phones as hearing from loved ones was something so crucial during our time there.

"We had been placing our trust in man and therefore our foundation was shaken when man failed us."

On July 5th, about one week after arriving in Guinea, we received an email that would prove to be one of, if not, the biggest challenges that we would face during our entire time in Guinea. The email was from our senior pastor. In it he shared that the church would only be supporting us with $300 a month. It was quite a shock to hear that they were only going to give us one quarter of what we had requested. Jenn and I were very hurt. Because things were already so demanding, Jenn's thought was, "Good! We'll just go back home." I knew that was not God's plan but I did not know how we were going to proceed. Our housing alone would cost over $200 a month. Apparently, there had been a major miscommunication. In my hurt, I sent an email expressing my thanks but also my surprise. The response to that email was not what I had hoped for and it quickly became apparent that this was not going to be an easy solution. Over the next few days, I came to realize that we were just going to have to rely on God for our finances as well. In my mind, I had known that all along, but when the rubber hit the road, I realized that my dependence had been on man and not on God.

Despite our immediate shock and hurt, the ordeal turned out to be a great lesson for us in trusting God. We had been placing our trust in man and therefore our foundation was shaken when man failed us. Sometimes there is a temptation to learn the wrong things from our experiences. There was a tendency to say, "Well, now I know who I can trust" or "I guess I will protect myself better next time." I do not believe this is the point of trials and it was not the lesson to learn from our situation. The trials are not usually to teach us more about people but more about God. Through each situation, we can say, "Wow! God is so gracious and so faithful. I will continue to place my hope in Him alone!"

YOUR SEARCH...

When have you experienced God's grace in the midst of a very difficult situation?

Is it easier to thank God for His deliverance or to complain in the trials? Why?

Take a minute to think back on all the times that God has encouraged you during a difficult time and thank Him for His grace and mercy.

"In this you greatly rejoice, though now for a little while you may have had to suffer grief in all kinds of trials. These have come so that your faith—of greater worth than gold, which perishes even though refined by fire—may be proved genuine and may result in praise, glory and honor when Jesus Christ is revealed." – 1 Peter 1:6-7

CHAPTER TWELVE
SETTLING IN?

Our week at the guesthouse ended up being about two weeks, as setting up our house took longer than expected. Pastor Pius had contacted us about two weeks before we arrived in Guinea to let us know that they he and others from his church had found the perfect place for us to live. From what we saw in the few pictures we were sent and from what we were told, it was a three-story home with five bedrooms. It looked great on the surface and sounded massive. Amazingly, it would only cost us about $200 a month. The first time that I saw the house in person, I was definitely impressed. Compared to anything we had ever lived in, it was absolutely massive! It must have been over 3000 square feet, with five balconies, five bedrooms, six bathrooms, three sitting areas, a kitchen, two storage closets, an office, and a garage! It definitely seemed like overkill. I knew we did not need this much space but smaller places, with only two or three rooms, were easily as much, and sometimes even more money than this.

Although it was big enough to be a castle, it was definitely not fit for king. We quickly discovered that it lacked most of the things that Americans usually expect in a home. Not only was it quite dirty on the inside, with lots of bugs and cobwebs, but there was also no water in the house and only sporadic electricity. It was like living in a giant, concrete warehouse. The kitchen consisted of a floating counter and a sink. There were no cupboards, shelves or appliances. Most of the faucets and fixtures in the bathrooms appeared to be broken or almost there. There was work to be done, and we did not have the money to do it. We knew that we had some tough decisions and a long road ahead of us. But looking on the bright side... we had a HUGE roof over our heads in a fairly nice and a safe neighborhood, with plenty of room for any visitors to come and visit!

"I had learned more about God in two weeks then I did in a year's time in the states."

Before moving into the place, we decided that I should spend a night there to see how things went and determine what else we needed to do before moving in. It was a rough night! Staying alone in a huge house in country you have never lived can be very scary. On top of that, there were noises throughout the night which kept me on my toes. Because of the heat, I had planned on sleeping without covers. That quickly changed when I began getting eaten alive by mosquitoes. I ended up hot and sweaty, underneath a sheet which I struggled to keep over every inch of my body. Based on that ridiculous night, we decided to borrow a tent and set it up inside the house. As a family, we slept all together in that tent for the first week or so at the house.

July 14, 2007

Tonight is our first night in our house. As I write this, I am sitting in a black, hot, mosquito-infested, house without running water. I just finished my first African bath – a bucket of cold water in the dark. I hate it here. What am I doing here? I can't handle it. I want to go home! The only pleasant thing at the moment is my sugar cookie scented candle. I am so glad I brought that!

Living in the house was quite challenging at times. After about a month of being in Guinea, I wrote the following outline of a typical day for my family:

> **MORNING:** We wake up at about 7:00 am, which is when the electricity shuts off...on a GOOD day. After a while, we head downstairs to prepare some sort of

breakfast. Due to a mostly broken stove, cereal is the easiest, though expensive at about $8 a box. We add to the cereal some powdered milk mix, which takes getting used to. At first, it tastes a lot like baby formula. Because of the price of cereal, we have been making a lot of eggs which are not too bad at about $2.00 a dozen, and pancakes and syrup from scratch. After that, I head outside to gather the rain water that we have hopefully collected during the night. We cart the large containers upstairs to use for bath water, and toilet flushing. Some goes in the kitchen for doing the dishes. Then I take some of the water and begin to filter it with our hand pump for drinking water. The rest is set aside for hand washing our clothes during the day. We usually do some shopping for food each day. This usually includes multiple stops since you usually can't find everything you need at one place. Without a car, we catch taxis everywhere. This can be quite interesting, especially with children. Just the other day we had three people in the front of the small Corolla and four adults with four children in the back seat! You read right, that is a total of 11 people in a small sedan!

AFTERNOON: The afternoons have become a great time for ministry. We are quickly becoming the place to hang out for the neighborhood children. We had about ten of them all playing with the kids' toys the other day. I have also had some great times sharing the gospel with a Muslim man in our neighborhood. We have had great discussions, and I am praying that he will accept the good news of Jesus Christ. At the beginning of the week, one of our local friends took me around and introduced me to all the neighbors. It was neat to see how relational people are. They were so welcoming to us. Three times a week we have a teacher who comes to the house for about an hour and a half to teach us French. It is very helpful to be learning French from a local since it varies from the French spoken in France. Another great thing is that he only charges about $1.50 an hour. There may also be an opportunity for us to learn Susu, which is the language in Mambia, around September.

EVENING: At the end of the day, we bathe the children in a small plastic tub usually in our front yard. We call it swimming so that they don't mind the cold water as much. After we get the kids to sleep under their mosquito nets, we take our "showers". This is done in the complete dark except for one small flashlight. We stand in the tub and pour cold rain water over us with a small water pitcher. If it is a great night we have some lights and electricity at 7:00 pm. At least half of the nights this does not happen until about midnight though. Since we are in the dark after about 7:00, we usually head to bed by about 8:30. It takes a while to fall asleep as we listen to the thousands of frogs outside of our bedroom. They seem to argue with each other in about four different languages. Sometimes Jenn thinks she can understand what some of them are saying! In addition to the normal tossing and turning, we normally wake up at least once more, which is at about 5:00 am when the local mosque shouts the call to prayer over their loudspeaker. (This takes place five times each day.)

The challenges that come with living in a new and very different culture were everywhere. Sometimes we learned and grew by watching others and sometimes we learned from those who had already experienced this new lifestyle. Other times, however, we had to learn lessons the old fashioned way...by mistake!

One day as we waited for a taxi, we spotted a chameleon on the side of the road. Excited at the potential of having one as a pet, we carefully picked it up. It was fairly docile and did not seem to mind being carried. We then hopped into a taxi which already had a few people in it. As we entered, someone saw the lizard. They screamed and the people in the car began quickly climbing out, noticeably disturbed. The taxi driver would not let us ride with the lizard. We later found out that many people are scared of them. Some even think they are demon-possessed because their eyes move in different directions at the same time!

There were other lessons that our time in America had already prepared us for. For example, having received many spam emails before moving to Guinea, I was fully aware of how these internet scams worked and the importance of not giving out personal information. What I was not prepared for was experiencing one of these emails in person.

I am sure that many of you have received one of those emails...someone from Nigeria has millions of dollars and wants you to have it. They will happily send it to you once you give them your contact information and a small fee to "free" up the funds. Well, one day I met a man who went on and on about how wonderful it was that we were working in the country. He then proceeded to tell me that he had a few hundred thousand dollars at his disposal. He had been looking for the right person to give this money to. Obviously, I was that man! I felt very honored, yet slightly skeptical. I told him that we would gladly receive the money and put it to good use.

"Okay. I will bring them money here from Sierra Leone and let you know when it arrives," he said.

For the next few days, I waited patiently for my newfound fortune to arrive. A few days later he found me and explained that there was a bit of a problem. I would still get the money but unfortunately the person driving the car full of money had stopped short of the border because of the police checkpoint. Surely they would find the money and confiscate it. If I could just give him a few hundred dollars, he could go pay of the police to let the car through. I don't think he had completely thought this explanation out in advance.

"I've got an idea" I said. "Why don't you just grab a few hundred dollars out of the back of the trunk and pay the police off with that!"

This caught him a bit off guard, and he tried to recover by saying that the police would see them and then it would all be over. Since he had originally explained how God had led him to me, I told him not to worry. We would just keep praying and if God wanted me to have the money, the police would let them through the checkpoint. If not, then I guess it was just not meant to be! The man left pretty disappointed that his get-rich-quick scheme had not worked out. We laughed about that story for many months after that!

Despite the culture shock and the difficulty of trying to adjust, we were beginning to get along quite well. The people were very kind. Everyone loved the kids. Selah even received a marriage proposal by a teenage boy who had joined us for lunch. (This became a common occurrence for us, as there are many people in Guinea who would love to marry an American and travel to the States.) Cedar was enjoying his time because he could see boats on the ocean and Selah was enjoying the coconut trees. They also both loved the lizards everywhere. For me however, this had already become the most difficult thing I had ever done, yet, at the same time, I had learned more about God in two weeks then I did in a year's time in the states. The biggest lesson I learned during that first month is how God answers prayers and how He provides when He is all you have.

YOUR SEARCH...

What adventures have you been on that have taken you well out of your comfort zone?

During that time, what did you learn about yourself? What did you learn about God?

Make a list of ways you have become too comfortable and some practical ways that you can allow yourself to be stretched.

"But he said to me, 'My grace is sufficient for you, for my power is made perfect in weakness." Therefore, I will boast all the more gladly about my weaknesses, so that Christ's power may rest on me. That is why, for Christ's sake, I delight in weaknesses, in insults, in hardships, in persecutions, in difficulties. For when I am weak, then I am strong." – 2 Corinthians 12:9-10

CHAPTER THIRTEEN
MEET THE FAMILY

About three weeks after arriving in Guinea, we were able to take our first trip out to Mambia as a family. It was a long-awaited journey, and I was excited for Jenn and the kids to see the place that we had been called to. Staying in the city of Conakry can be a bit overwhelming at times. The crowds of people, flurry of cars and heaps of trash can leave you feeling a bit claustrophobic. Having been to Mambia before, I knew that the cleaner air and beautiful scenery would be a welcome change for my family. I was eager to introduce them to the people of Mambia as well. Mambia was where things changed for me during my first trip to Guinea. It is where my fear and depression was replaced with anticipation for what God had in store. It is where the calling on my life had been confirmed. I wanted my wife to feel that same encouragement and share in the excitement of seeing her dream become a reality. We knew that staying in the capital city was just a starting point. The real work and our purpose would be found in this small village that not many had even heard of.

♦♦♦

July 20, 2007

We went to Mambia yesterday. The drive there was beautiful. Very green. We saw many waterfalls and streams. It seemed like Costa Rica or, like Selah said, Hawaii. It was not how I had pictured Africa. When we got to the village, we met with some elders in a grass hut. About 60 villagers surrounded us. It was a little chaotic as the translations made it take quite a while to communicate. The elders asked us right away why we would pick Mambia. "There are 33 towns between here and Conakry. Why would you come to Mambia?" We shared with them how I had seen Mambia in a dream. It is so amazing to be at a place I saw and to see how they are so accepting. It was very neat. We asked them what was something they needed, and they explained how they needed drinkable water. They have three public wells but one is very far and the other two are broken. We talked about channeling water from a nearby stream. They want us to spend the night. They said that is how friendships are formed. They are very accepting of us. Afterwards, we passed out biscuits to the children. They attacked us like piranhas. I'm glad we bought them a treat.

Once again, we were welcomed with open arms in the village. They truly wanted us to make their home, our new home! Although we knew that we were not quite ready for that big of a change, we knew that soon we would be spending quite a bit of time there. During this visit, we were reminded of their ever-present need of water. As we returned to the capital, we felt energized and excited for the future. Though still unsure of the details we knew two things that we needed to start planning for. First, we needed to explore ways to bring water to the people. And second, we needed to begin spending more time in the village.

"Mambia was where things changed for me during my first trip to Guinea."

During our trips out to Mambia, we were introduced to a common practice for the locals. Apparently, they will give foreigners a Guinean name for various reasons. Many times they do this because the foreigner's name is too hard to pronounce. This is also seen as a sign of friendship and trust. I was the first to be "named." The chief of the village gave me the name Moussa Sylla, which is also the name of one of his sons. To this day, many people in the country only know me by that name. Cedar also received a Susu name from one of the men there. A young man with one leg took a liking to him and said he would like to call him Alasan Sylla because that is his name. In Susu, this is called a toxoman (tō-hō-mon), or a namesake because the one was named after the other. Jenn's Susu name is Fanta and was given to her by the wife of a former Prime Minister of Guinea. Selah's Susu name is Salematu and was given to her by a good missionary friend who has worked with the Susu for many years.

Cedar and his toxoman, Alasan Sylla

This practice reminds me of the times in the Bible that people receive a new name. Often when God called someone to begin a new work or start on a new path, he gave them a new name. This was the case of Abram who became Abraham, Sarai who became Sarah, Jacob who became Israel, and Simon who became Peter. Each of these changes was done as a confirmation that God was doing something unique through that person's life. Just as it was a reassurance of God's plan for them, we saw this as a testimony of God's direction in our own lives.

YOUR SEARCH...

When was the last time you saw God answer one of your prayers?

What are some prayers that you have right now that have yet to be answered?

Ask God to give you patience as you wait for Him to answer your prayers in His timing and in His way.

"Yet the Lord longs to be gracious to you; he rises up to show you compassion. For the Lord is a God of justice. Blessed are all who wait for him!" – Isaiah 30:18

CHAPTER FOURTEEN

MIRACLES HAPPEN

I have always heard that there are many miracles taking place in other countries. For some reason or another, not many North Americans ever see a miraculous sign or wonder. I believe that one reason for this is that we have so many safeguards in America. In a sense, God does not need to do a miracle because we have it covered by an insurance plan. The comforts of the States have left many of us without an apparent need to fervently cry out to the Lord. The things we think of as trials, are often so trivial. For example, before living in Guinea, I remember getting so impatient waiting for a stoplight to turn green. God forbid that it take more than 3 minutes to let me through! On my return to the states, I remember waiting at a stoplight, thinking, "Praise the Lord that we have rules on our roads and that there is electricity to keep these stoplights on." While in Africa we saw God move in some mighty and miraculous ways. As we had no other option but to call and wait on Him, we experienced the power of God in a way we never had before. Here are a few journal entries of some of those miraculous events...

◆◆◆

August 5, 2007

At church today there was a guest speaker. I enjoyed the message. One of the things he talked about was that God was going to bless us and provide for us. He encouraged us to ask God to do that out loud. At first, I was thinking we did not really need anything; especially compared to most of the people there. I remembered that we were almost completely out of money though and that we were going to have to figure out how to get more money on Monday. I thought about this and told myself that God could provide on Monday, but there wasn't anyone in Africa that was going to give us money today. Despite these thoughts I asked God in confidence to meet our needs. Later that day as we were doing some cleaning at home, I came across a money belt of mine that felt heavy. When I opened it up, I was shocked to find $700 in it! Jenn and I both thought we were completely out of money and could not figure out how we had misplaced $700. God really did meet our needs!

August 6, 2007

Today I had quite an experience. On our way to do email at the CMA guesthouse, I almost lost my laptop computer and digital camera. I hopped out of a taxi with Jenn and the kids and left my *backpack in the taxi. As he drove away I realized what happened and tried to chase him down the road to no avail. When I realized he was gone, I started to panic. Just then another taxi pulled up behind me. I hurriedly climbed in and in broken French tried to tell him what happened. As we followed I kept my eye out for the taxi. Suddenly, my driver pulled over just as I saw the other taxi ahead waiting at an intersection. I tried to tell my driver that I needed him to hurry. He pointed back and said something. Presumably someone in the back was getting out. I knew I had to make a run for it. I jumped out of the cab and began running down the middle of the road in the rain yelling, "Chauffeur!" which means driver (duh) and waving my arms violently. As I came within about 300 feet, he began to pull away. People on the side of the road saw me and tried yelling to the driver too. Finally, he looked in his rear view mirror and saw me and pulled over. My bag was still safe inside the cab. Praise the Lord!!! God is merciful! As I walked back down the road, I passed the taxi that I had jumped from. The reason he had pulled over was because he had a flat tire. If I had stayed in it, everything would have been gone and I would probably never have seen my laptop again!*

August 12, 2007

So...the day that I have been on my knees asking God for has arrived...and so much earlier than I ever could have imagined! Last night I had the pleasure of leading a Fula man to the Lord! Every night for about the past two weeks I have been sharing the gospel with him. He speaks a little broken English and I speak a little broken French. Four days ago, we invited him to church with us, and he said he would go. He had never been to church before in his life. We waited for him on Sunday, praying like crazy. that he would show up. Well he did, praise the Lord! After service, he said he wanted to talk to me that night. So that night when I saw him, he began to share how much he enjoyed church. He said that he had such peace and joy in his heart as soon as he entered the church. He believed and accepted everything that was shared. He said that in his religion (Muslim), they do not do what they believe. He said he wanted to live as a Christian, and he wants me to teach him everything I can about the Bible. The one problem he said is that his father and family will not accept his choice. We are praying that he can be strong and that he will grow daily in the Lord.

"She called me on the phone crying, 'I want to go home!"

Our entire time in Guinea was a miracle. Each day that we were there was a testimony to God's grace. The fact that I was able to lead a man to the Lord even with a HUGE language barrier was proof that the Holy Spirit was working. Our guard, who gave his life to the Lord, began attending church services through another missionary friend. It was there that he decided to be baptized. We were very excited and as a family attended the service. It was great to see him make this decision. At the baptism he shared his testimony, and we were truly blessed to be a part of the whole thing.

We realized that there were many people who played a huge role in these miracles. Without the prayers and support of others, we would never have had this opportunity. Never undervalue the responsibility you have to pray for and support those who share the gospel across the world. I truly believe that God uses and rewards those who stay behind just as much as those who go. There are no small roles in the kingdom of God!

"The share of the man who stayed with the supplies is to be the same as that of him who went down to the battle. All will share alike." – 2 Samuel 30:24

The fact that Jenn stayed in Guinea even after having seven worms in her skin was another miracle. You read that right. Jenn had worms in her skin. One day she found what looked like a pimple only to find that it continued to grow and began to cause a lot of pain in her leg. A few days later, as she squeezed it, a small maggot crawled out of the hole! She was mortified. "I want to go home!" she cried when she called me on the phone. She told me what was going on and that I needed to hurry home. When I arrived, she had me examine the rest of her body and we found that six more of these creatures were living in her skin. On close examination of my own skin, I also had three worms in my skin as well. After consulting some friends, we were told that the best way to remove the worms was to cover the hole with Vaseline so that it could not breathe. It would then move its way to the surface of the skin where it could be removed. Needless to say, that was a pretty rough day! Jenn still has a scar on her leg from the largest one.

After living in the capital for about three months, we made the decision to move into an apartment. There were many reasons for the move. One of the biggest reasons though was that it was less expensive than the home we were in. Due to the smaller size, it was also easier to maintain making it a better option for us, since we planned to spend more and more time in the village of Mambia. The apartment was still in Conakry and not too far from the house where we had been living. It was centrally located, which made shopping without a vehicle much easier. We also had some great neighbors. They were missionaries as well, who had spent years ministering to the Susu people.

Though the apartment was much nicer than the previous house, we still had struggles. Electricity was a consistent problem. I had hooked up a few 12-volt light bulbs to a truck battery so that we could have some light in the house, but that only worked when we were able to charge the battery with city power, which was sometimes non-existent for multiple days at a time. When the battery was drained, we often used headlamps to see our way around. This worked fine, most of the time...

One night I was preparing to eat the last few lemon squares which I had made from a box mix the day before. I pulled the leftover bars from our refrigerator, which was basically a storage container since electricity was scarce. Heading to the couch in the living room, I unwrapped the foil surrounding the bars and took my first few bites of the sweet, lemony goodness. Suddenly, something did not seem quite right. I directed my headlamp down towards the foil. To my dismay, there were hundreds of tiny ants on the bars and in the foil! I was not excited about the added protein and quickly threw the rest of the bars away.

I hated getting rid of the dessert, especially since it was a rare treat. It had come in a care package from someone in the States. These packages were so encouraging to receive but unfortunately, they did not always make it to us. Mail was unreliable. On days we did receive a package, we went to retrieve it from the post office and would often notice that it had been opened and gone through. We were even told at times that we could not take the package unless we paid some money to the postal workers. We realized that sending and receiving packages was another thing we had taken for granted in America.

Around that time, we also began to study the Susu language with a small group of other missionaries. It was a huge blessing to be invited to this class which was something that was not part of the normal calendar. God's timing was perfect! We took the class every Monday and Thursday for a few hours and then did some lessons throughout the week. Since Susu is the official language in the capital as well as Mambia, learning the language was very beneficial.

Mambia was not our only place of service or focus. There were other ministry opportunities that often presented themselves. One of those came when we were asked to help with the youth group for missionary kids in Conakry. We had about 20 junior and senior high students in the group. The pastor who was meeting with them every other Saturday night had recently returned to the States on furlough. Having done many years of youth ministry, it was a joy to be involved in something familiar and in our native language!

Evidence of the cultural differences was everywhere. One of the most striking differences was revealed in a conversation I had with a Muslim neighbor who could not understand why I would not beat my wife if she was disrespectful to me. For many of them, this is quite a normal practice because the Islamic holy book, the Quran, teaches them that this behavior is acceptable. I shared with this man how the way I treat my wife is influenced by the character of God. I told him that while the rest of the world says that we should repay evil with evil, Jesus told us to forgive one another. He seemed completely confused by the concept of turning the other cheek. We realized on a daily basis the need for people there to understand the love and forgiveness of Jesus so that they will also learn to forgive others.

In addition to the support we received from friends and family at home, I cannot say enough how much support we received from the missionary community in Guinea. From the daily calls, help with shopping and housework, encouragement and meals, we continually felt wrapped in love by those Christians living in Guinea. We were also blessed to be invited to two different retreats at the end of October 2017. The first was a women's retreat for Jenn and Selah. After that we all got to go to a retreat for missionaries working with the Susu people. They were both held on an island just off the coast of Conakry and our cost was covered completely by the churches sponsoring them. The island was quite beautiful and we had a very relaxing trip and a wonderful time getting to know those who were there with us. Most of all, we were humbled and amazed by the dedication these churches from America had.

They were willing to spend so much time, energy and money coming out to minister to not only those from their church, but to all the missionaries in the country! You could really tell how much they valued missionary work and how dedicated they were to reaching the lost.

YOUR SEARCH...
What ministry or ministries are you involved in currently?

What are some others areas where you might be able to demonstrate God's love to the world around you?

Look for small ways to be a blessing to others. Pray for open doors. Involve your family if you have one. When you do these things, you will experience the joy that comes from giving.

"In everything I did, I showed you that by this kind of hard work we must help the weak, remembering the words the Lord Jesus himself said: 'It is more blessed to give than to receive.'"
- Acts 20:35

CHAPTER FIFTEEN

THE PLAN REVEALED

Things continued to happen in miraculous ways all around us. From our safety and protection to our provision, we continued to see God's hands working. Unfortunately though, we still had no clue what we He wanted us to do in the country. We were praying for more specifics and God was faithful to answer that prayer...

PAUL'S JOURNAL

August 22, 2007

Last night was very good. Jenn and I began talking about our future in Guinea and different possibilities of what God might want us to do. The more we talked the more we realized that it seemed that God was leading us to begin some sort of Bible school or Bible college here. We talked about the connections that we have and we talked about getting other Calvary Chapels involved. We started to realize that we have so many opportunities to begin something like this. It was completely in line with how God had gifted and prepared us. We decided to just spend some time praying about it and surrender it to the Lord. As we were praying, both of us felt more confirmation from the Lord that it was the right direction to proceed with. We really got excited and both really felt like this is it. This is where God is taking us. We realized that there could be a great opportunity for youth at Westbrook to get trained and eventually serve over here. We believe that many people here would be very interested in attending something like this. We believe that the next step might be talking to Calvary Chapel and discussing the process of beginning something like this. We think a great way to start would be to do a history class. It could be "From Moses to David". Something like that would be very interesting to many of the Muslims because the Quran talks about some of those men briefly. We definitely want to move in this direction and pray that God would open and close doors as needed.

November 16, 2007

We had an awesome time in Mambia today. There were so many cool things that happened. It was neat to think that we were going to go on Tuesday but Michel (the driver we used regularly) could only do today. When we arrived we met with the chief as well as some other leaders. I also got to meet my Toxoman for the first time. Shortly after *that we met with the Sous Prefecture of Mambia. He said he was taking us to Kindia, so off we went. On the way we picked up another leader and met a few others. Once we arrived in Kindia, we entered a government complex and were introduced to some very important people. It was the Prefecture of the entire Kindia region as well as some other important officials. They "just happened" to be gathered together because the Prime Minister of Guinea is coming to see them tomorrow. He asked us why we came to Mambia and what our plans in Mambia were. We explained Jenn's dream and our desire to help with water and teach the Bible.*

He was very accepting and said we were very welcome. He introduced us to the man in charge of all community projects and religious organizations in Kindia. He said that we should be in regular communication with him when we desire to work or begin programs. On the way back to Mambia we stopped in Ibraham's home town which is where the bauxite plant is. We met his family and also met the man who is in charge of the bauxite relations. I asked him about the company helping with the water situation in Mambia, and he said it is in the plans but would not happen for at least two or three more years. When we talked about this later, everyone said that more than likely this would never happen because they still have not done the first projects that they were supposed to do.

After we left, we went back to the Sous Prefecture's house in Mambia. He prepared a quick meal for us and we ate with him. After the meal, he said that he was very happy to have us in Mambia. He said that even though 99% of the people in Mambia are Muslim, the children are the future and that we could teach and bring up the youth to follow Christianity! He said whatever it is that we desire to do, we should do it.

We were absolutely blown away by the offer to teach children to become Christian. It was an unprecedented invitation and one that we could not ignore. This government official, who might be compared to a State Governor in America, had no idea that we both studied to be teachers. He had no knowledge of our heart for and experience with the youth. The way that he welcomed us and opened the door gave us such confidence that the Lord was truly going to do some big things in the village of Mambia. We still did not have all the answers but suddenly our direction became much clearer. We knew that we were going to begin teaching children and ministering to the youth.

"He showed me the scars on his body from sleeping in the prison beds."

On the way home that day, we had a great conversation with our friend, Ibraham, who had accompanied us on the trip. He said that it would be very difficult for him to become a Christian because of his family. However, he also said that he would, if we wanted him to, even if his family rejected him. We told him that it needed to be his choice and to just pray and let God show him what is true.

Around that same time, that we met a man who runs a small Christian school in the capital. We got to visit the school and even taught at it one week. There were about 35 kids from ages 6 to about 10. A couple of them were orphans. The majority of the children were from Muslim families who could not otherwise afford a private school. The school, which was basically a covered driveway, was free for the kids. All the teaching was done in English and included all subjects with a strong emphasis on the Bible. This encounter proved to be very encouraging as it gave us a picture of what might be possible in the future.

Another ministry opportunity that I had in the capital of Conakry was visiting the youth in jail. One of the missionaries there went every week to teach basketball to the boys there and he invited me to join him. The first time I went out I had a great time sharing the gospel with a fourteen-year-old boy. He was separated from his family in Sierra Leone when he was six and ended up in Guinea in a refugee camp. After that he got caught by the police for trespassing and was put in this prison. He showed me the scars on his body from sleeping in the prison beds. They were given bunk beds that basically had chicken coop wire where the mattresses would have gone. Seeing these young men in such horrible conditions made my heart break for them and made me all the more intent on sharing Christ with them.

There were many times when I saw people open to hearing the gospel. Despite their willingness to listen and even admit what they saw as truth, there was often great hesitancy in accepting Christ as their Savior. One example of this was with a young man who was our neighbor at our first house in Conakry. After spending time with us and getting to know our family, he attended church with us occasionally. He even made some amazing statements about the truth being found in Christianity. He said, however, becoming a Christian would cause him to face a lot of persecution from his family. It was quite discouraging at times to see people who recognized the truth but allowed the oppressive culture to dictate their choices. It continues to be a prayer of ours that people in these situations would have the strength to stand for the truth in the midst of hardship rather than living a lie in peace.

Sometimes we felt discouraged during our time in Guinea due to the fact that we did not have a specific ministry focus. Now, don't get me wrong, I don't think that people need a specific ministry in life. I think that is a philosophy that we have adapted in many churches which is not necessarily biblical. We often hear Christians asking each other what their ministry is or where they are serving. This can create a mindset that you are not fully living out your calling if you are just being a Christian at work and at home. Colossians 3:23-24 makes it clear that whatever we do should be done as work for the Lord. Our goal is to honor God in all things even when we do not see the fruit or feel like we are making a difference. That being said, it is definitely easier though to move forward and elicit the help of others when you have a goal in mind. For us, that specific ministry began to take shape after we had believed the Lord was calling us to start some sort of Bible school. It was then confirmed after meeting with the Sous-Prefe in Mambia. At that point, we knew what our focus was going to be but still were not sure how and when it would come about. Through various circumstances, we began to believe that local Guinean Christians would play an important part. God had already orchestrated divine appointments with people who were doing similar things in Guinea.

As November 2007 came to a close, we began to prepare for our return to California. Up until that point we had often questioned how long we would stay in Guinea. We considered that we might move back to California in December. Was it God's plan all along for us to go solely for the purpose of being stretched and experiencing personal growth? Was His desire that we learn to step out in faith and in the process encourage others to do the same? This thought was short-lived however.

We were so blown away by the doors that God had opened. We knew the work was just beginning. Seeing all the God had done so far, it was obvious that our time in Guinea was just starting. As comforting as the thought of returning home for good was, we knew it was not the right time. God had not only given us a burden for the people but also a joy in serving Him there, despite the difficulties. This time, we booked round trip tickets. I knew that Jenn was having a very tough time and that there was a good possibility that she would not want to go back once we were in America again but, thankfully, the open door we were given to start a school helped convince her that we were not finished. We would return to Guinea after visiting family and friends for about six weeks. And we knew what our plan was when we returned. The first goal was to begin spending more time with and discipling the Guinean Christians that we felt God was placing in our path and the second goal was to start teaching the Bible in Mambia.

YOUR SEARCH...

When you look back on your life, what areas do you see that God was preparing you for what you would do later on?

What situations have you experienced that have built the most character in your life?

Think about the mundane things that you are experiencing in your life right now. Allow yourself to embrace them as an opportunity to develop Godly character.

"Not only so, but we rejoice in our sufferings, because we know that suffering produces perseverance; perseverance, character; and character, hope." – Romans 5:3-4

CHAPTER SIXTEEN

FURLOUGH

The word furlough refers to a time of temporary release from one's duties or particular situation. For us, returning to America for a short time, provided a much needed break from the challenges of living overseas. During this time though, we experienced something we had not yet: reverse culture shock. It's what happens when you return home after being in a completely different culture for a long time. What used to be so familiar, now feels like a brand new experience. Things that you had taken for granted up until that point, become novelties. Walking into a Target for the first time since leaving California, took us by surprise. What overwhelmed the most was actually the aroma. The wonderful scents of cleaners, candles and perfumes filled our nostrils. It was so foreign from what we were now used to. There, in Guinea, most of the scents we experienced were those produced by bodies!

"We suddenly realized how easy it is for missionaries to become judgmental of other people."

Our view of traffic lights had also changed immensely. In the past, waiting for more than two minutes at a red light drove us to frustration! We would start wondering if something was wrong with the light and begin looking for alternative routes. Having experienced traffic in a country without visible traffic laws, a place where most drivers do whatever they want, we now had a new appreciation for these lights. We were so thankful for the order and sanity that they provided!

Our time home was fulfilling and refreshing. In addition to spending time with loved ones, I was also able to meet with some leaders at our church and share our frustration with the way the relationship had deteriorated. We wanted to be supported financially as well as emotionally and spiritually. Unfortunately, except for some key friends and family members, we felt mostly abandoned by our home church. The meeting went quite well though, and they asked us to forgive them for not being a spiritual support to us. They requested that I begin sending them monthly updates about what was going on in my life personally, beyond the general monthly newsletter, which I agreed to do. They also invited me to share on an upcoming Wednesday night, about our first six months in Guinea.

Despite the encouragement we felt in returning home, we had also begun to feel a strange disconnect from the lifestyle we had left. It was surprising to see that happen in such a short amount of time. We suddenly realized how easy it is for missionaries to become judgmental of other people. Coming off of the mission field, there can be a subconscious expectation that others see the world the way that you see it, even though many of them have never seen the world. It was only by the grace of God that my family had our eyes opened to see beyond the borders of prosperity and comfort and into the needs of the world outside of our bubble. We had experienced God in ways that we never could have imagined.

We were hit hard with the selfishness and vanity of the American culture upon our return. Laziness and complacency seemed to be the earmarks of the American church as a whole. In Guinea, we watched in amazement as people fought over the first scriptures and Bible stories they had ever seen. Our new outlook gave us more than just a heart for the lost. It also stirred in us a desire to see more Christians step out and be used as broken vessels, just as we had. I do not place all the blame on Christians in America for this apparent lack of involvement, rather, I desire to see them grow in their faith by expanding their worldview and life experiences.

During this time, we also became more aware of how different our view of "missions" had become. While at home, we spoke with a few people on different occasions, that had the desire to go to another country to share the gospel. Our counsel to them was to pursue what God had placed in their hearts while allowing the Holy Spirit to guide and direct them. The advice that they heard from friends and family however, often centered more on staying put until they had specific direction and more training. Although these differences may not be crucial to one's faith, they had become an important issue for us. We wanted others to experience the same joy and growth that we had experienced by taking a step of faith, rather than waiting in comfort for some supernatural sign that might never come. Besides this, scripture makes it clear that we have ALL been called to reach the lost. Do we really need more "revelation" than the Great Commission?

"Therefore go and make disciples of all nations, baptizing them in the name of the Father and of the Son and of the Holy Spirit, and teaching them to obey everything I have commanded you." – Matthew 28:19-20

Christian men and women frequently make decisions about their jobs, schooling, purchases and relationships with little to no caution from church leaders or with spiritual counsel. I have heard on many occasions, someone share how they are going to get a new car, a new home or change their job. Almost every time, the response was something along the lines of "That's great!" or "Praise the Lord!" Rarely, if ever, does someone respond "Did the Lord give you confirmation on that?" or "Perhaps you should be faithful where you are before making a decision like that." When someone feels led to become a missionary though, suddenly we have a checklist to make sure that they are truly called by God to go. The decision to spend frivolously on earthly things is applauded but passion to see the gospel spread is met with cautionary advice. Maybe we have this a bit backwards! I believe it is better to risk running into a closed door than to never get off of the couch! Do not let ANYTHING keep you from passionately pursuing God and stepping out in faith.

YOUR SEARCH...

How does God's view of the lost vary from your own?

When was the last time you openly shared your belief in God with another person?

Write a list of things that break your heart or that you are passionate about. Ask God if there are ways you can use that passion to serve as His ambassador to a hurting world.

"We are therefore Christ's ambassadors, as though God were making his appeal through us. We implore you on Christ's behalf: Be reconciled to God." – 2 Corinthians 5:20

CHAPTER SEVENTEEN
NIGHT ONE

W e arrived back in Guinea at the end of January 2008. This time we had a companion. Jenn's sister, Laura, accompanied us for a little over a week. I cannot tell you what a blessing it was to have someone sacrifice their time and money to learn firsthand what we were experiencing. When you are living in Guinea, despite your best efforts to treat someone like a tourist, they are bound to see the tremendous poverty and difficulties in the country. Although we wanted Laura to have a good time, there is definitely a feeling of encouragement when someone can understand and appreciate the challenges that you are facing.

After Laura returned to America, we began to focus our attention on two main goals. The first was to spend more time with Pepe, one of our local friends and partners in the ministry. Pepe was someone we met at the Nigerian church when we first arrived in Guinea. He was asked by the church leaders to come alongside and help us in any way he could. Usually this involved maintenance and construction at our house as well as some impromptu French lessons.

During the many days I spent with Pepe, we became close friends. His faith and integrity were a constant source of inspiration. To this day, one of his favorite sayings is "By the grace of God." Anytime we discuss plans, he follows it up with that statement knowing that whatever we do is ultimately under God's control. In addition to his humility, he is hard-working, full of integrity and passionate about honoring God. Needless to say, he was and continues to be a tremendous blessing in my life.

The second goal was to spend more time in Mambia. This proved to be another step of faith in itself. We knew that the village had no electricity and that it was very time consuming to obtain water. The "house" that we were offered to stay in was a hut about twenty feet in diameter with one large bed in the middle. We also did not have a reliable vehicle and wrestled through how we would get back and forth to Mambia. Food was an issue too, since there weren't any actual stores near Mambia. The most feasible option seemed to be packing a cooler with perishable items, but even that would only last a few days. In the end we decided to proceed slowly. Our plan was to start by going out for one night, then two or three nights and then for about a week at a time.

February 12, 2008

We had a great time in Mambia today. Ibraham, Pius, Regina, Pepe and Bah all went with us. Our goals were two-fold. We wanted to start making measurements for a water supply and also determine if we could stay out there a week from this Friday and what we would need for that stay. When we discussed that we wanted to stay a night with the Sous-Prefe and the chief, they said that they had a different place than the guesthouse for us to stay. They said it would work better for us because it was bigger. It has four or five rooms in it. The Sous-Prefe said that it would be good for us because we could have visitors stay with us, and we could also use a room to teach the Bible and worship! With this new development of a bigger house to stay in and more encouragement to start some sort of Bible study, we were very excited to try our first night of village living. However, we decided that we would not attempt it without Pepe. Don't think that we were fearless just because we moved to Africa! Once he agreed to accompany us we began purchasing items that we needed and making the necessary arrangements to spend a night in Mambia.

February 23, 2008

WOW! There is so much to share. I just hope I can remember it all. It started yesterday morning.

We took the Span's car and headed out for our first overnight stay in Mambia. When we arrived in Mambia we met with the Sous Prefe and told him that we would like to set up our house. He introduced us to some youth and a couple leaders. He told them that we had a message to share with them and that they should listen to us and make their choice since they will be the future of Mambia. After that they gave us the keys, and we got a room for Pepe and a room for us set up. We left two mosquito nets, two screens, two mats, some small toys, a broom, a large bucket, a candle plate, a mosquito skin spray, a pot, and three coffee cups. After meeting with some new people, we headed out with the Sous Prefe to look at the water situation in more detail. They have four wells that we found. Two of them are missing the pump parts which were stolen, one of them is a working well at the hospital and the other one is a private well at the Sous-Prefe's house. We were informed that they were going to have a welcome for us that evening, so we hung out at our house. Finally, at about 8:30 people started showing up. By about 9:30 they finally got started with loud music, singing and dancing. They had about four percussionists, two singers and then a lot of the ladies who came did the dancing. They finally wrapped things up at about 10:30. Pepe and I stayed up praying until about midnight. The whole night was really quite an experience.

Local musician playing a balafon

Our first overnight trip to Mambia went very well. The house that was temporarily given to us by the villagers was basically a small school. There were about six rooms. Two of them even had chalkboards on the walls. The place needed a lot of work, but we could see lots of potential. The little "welcome" party was unlike anything we had ever experienced. Apparently the chief had hired an authentic group of musicians from a nearby village. There were two guys with these amazing xylophone things (balafons), two singers and three guys with some unique drums. We obviously had different ideas of bedtime since the concert began at 9:30 p.m. while our children attempted to sleep inside one of the rooms!

The next day during our tour of the local public school, we got to greet the 250 younger kids and about 100 older kids that were in attendance. Each classroom was extremely basic. There was a wall used as a chalkboard and lines of wooden desks with four or five kids squeezed together on each one. The little hospital in the village was not much more sophisticated. There were some basic supplies and some outdated equipment, but they lacked experienced and trained personnel.

"Muslims from Mecca pass through Mambia on their way to the big cities but none of them ever stop here."

We really enjoyed our first night in the village and were even more convinced of the need to spend as much time there as possible. There was an open door, and we needed to take it. The living conditions were by no means pleasant, but they seemed manageable. In retrospect, I think God tricked us! He knew that first night had to go well so that we would make plans to stay longer.

We looked forward to our trips to Mambia. The village life was much different from the city. Although it was challenging, it was quiet and clean. The landscape was inviting and the people were always so excited to see us. After one of the local leaders encouraged a group of youth who had gathered, to listen to the message we would be sharing with them, he then showed us to the house where they wanted us to stay. Upon arrival, he continued by saying that it was a great place to teach the Bible and to worship. He also said that he was sure that we would want to go out into the village, share our message with people and invite them to join us for worship. This was absolutely amazing coming from a Muslim! We were quite confused, yet elated by the heartfelt welcome.

"Muslims from Mecca pass through Mambia on their way to the big cities, but none of them ever stop here" he said. He also seemed quite amazed that these Christians came all the way from California specifically for them! Our desire to provide people in the village with clean drinking water was still alive and strong. In fact, staying in the village for days at a time showed us just how difficult it truly was to be without an easily accessible source of water. In the beginning, we were thinking that piping water from a nearby stream would be the best way to help Mambia with their water situation. After receiving the bid however, we began looking into doing wells instead. The hope was that the cost would be much lower and there would be many less potential problems this way. Our long-term plan was to dig about four wells and repair two existing wells that were currently broken. We determined that the cost to dig a well by hand would be around $2000. We began sharing this need with our contacts in an effort to raise the necessary funds.

YOUR SEARCH...

Can you describe a time when an unexpected change in your plans ended up being a good thing?

Why do you think we get upset or discouraged when things do not work out how we plan them?

When your plans suddenly change, make a mental list of things that God might be doing or things that you might learn through those changes.

"In his heart a man plans his course, but the Lord determines his steps." – Proverbs 16:9

CHAPTER EIGHTEEN

BATS IN HELL

After a few more day trips, we finally decided on our first three-day stay over in Mambia. From the onset, we felt that the enemy was trying to distract us from going. We faced obstacles and setbacks at almost every turn. It started the night before we left, when Cedar developed a fever. As we got our stuff together in the morning, we found out that Pepe would not be able to go with us. Instead, he would be sending his brother. By the time we got out there, Jenn's back was in a great deal of pain due to the very rough ride in the car. Though feeling discouraged, we powered through each challenge.

Upon arrival, we set out to make our humble abode as livable as possible. One night in the village is easier to get through knowing that you will be leaving the next day. Preparing for more than that meant we needed a plan for meals, showers and privacy. For us, this involved trying to put together a make-shift sink in the room we were using as a kitchen, so that we could wash and prepare meals.

It also consisted of trying to clean and fix the "outhouse" so that it was usable. The current set up was three side-by-side stalls. Each stall was about three feet by five feet. Two of the stalls had hole in the middle with a six inch raised platform. The platform had places for your feet on either side. These were used to stand on while you squatted over the hole when relieving yourself. The third stall was empty except for a smaller hole in the middle for water to drain out of. This stall was used for washing yourself. Although using this place as our bathroom would be challenging, the bigger problem was that the room was less than six feet high which meant that we would have to hunch over every time we went in to any of the stalls. We made the decision to increase the height by about a foot and a half to solve the problem. It's not a phrase I use much, but I was definitely excited to be "raising the roof" that day!

The third project was to see if we could get rid of the bats, which we discovered had taken over the entire attic space, as well as several rooms in the building. Each project that we tried to tackle, felt like a futile attempt to catch the blowing wind. Despite our best efforts, there was almost nothing we could do to change the uncomortable living conditions out there. We had only a few small hand tools, nowhere to purchase supplies and our patience was disappearing quickly!

"outhouse"

"kitchen"

The first night was probably the worst night of our lives. The temperature of our room at 9:00 pm was about 85 degrees with about 100 percent humidity, and we had no electricity or fans to change that. During the night, Cedar's fever got worse. He woke up multiple times throughout the night and was even vomiting on occasion. The "bed" we slept on was an old mattress from a pull-out couch. Through the thin outer fabric, you could feel the poking of the straw with which it was made. The lack of comfort made sleeping on the concrete floor sound like a preferable option, and that is probably where I would have ended up, if it had not been for the fear of all the bugs that were in our room.

"We could hear their claws as they scratched eerily on the tin roof above us."

As we lay in the pitch black, I could not tell for certain if the bats were in the ceiling or if they actually in our room. Their fluttering and screeching sounded so close at times that I think I woke up swatting at the air on a few occasions. We could hear their claws as they scratched eerily on the tin roof above us. As if all of this was not enough, we were awakened numerous times throughout the night to the sound of what seemed to be someone throwing rocks at the metal roofing. The loud crashes came off like a shotgun and often jolted us right out of bed. In the morning, we discovered the culprit of the noise was actually a tree hanging over our house which was covered with hard green spheres about the size of a large gumball. These balls would fall onto the roof which a crash at about one to five minute intervals. Literally, the WORST... NIGHT... EVER!

April 19, 2008

Highly annoyed with the "ball tree." We asked Pepe if it bears any fruit.

"No" he said. "The balls are just seeds to make more trees."

"Is the tree for anything?" I asked, to which Pepe replied "firewood."

"Great," I'm thinking. "This cursed tree drops balls on my roof so that it can produce more of these awful trees."

"But it's almost finished dropping balls and then will come..." Paul and I waited in anticipation of something cool, but Pepe continued "...then will come these big, nasty caterpillars."

"WHAT?!" we said.

Pepe continued to emphasize the nastiness of these caterpillars and how they will drop all over. Paul and I cried, laughing and thinking how much we hated this tree and saw absolutely no point to its existence.

The next day, we continued our vain efforts to obtain some sort of comfort in this harsh environment. Jenn was very frustrated and concerned about Cedar. She mentioned that if Cedar continued to have a fever it might be best to return to the city in the morning instead of staying an extra day. The next night did not go any better. We had the same situation as the night before, but now Selah also had a fever. When we woke up in the morning, Jenn and I talked about what we were doing out there. We both realized that this was an attack of the enemy. There was a need for this village to hear the gospel and Satan did not want that to happen. At that point we made a choice. We decided that it was time to stop surviving and start serving. Comfort was obviously not coming anytime soon and since we were only there for a short time anyway, we might as well use it to be a blessing to others. Almost immediately after making that conscious choice to put others first, Selah and Cedar both started feeling better.

Based on our conversation with the Sous-Prefe months earlier, we decided we should start by ministering to the children. Pepe's brother, Alphons and I headed out to meet with the chief. We told him that we wanted to teach a Bible study to the children if they were willing to come and listen. He said that he would tell those in the village and send them to our house at about 4:00 that afternoon. We went back to the house to prepare for their arrival. Well 4:00 came and went and no one had arrived. We waited another hour and still no one. Another hour went by, then another. By 8:00 in the evening, we still did not have one visitor at the house. We were once again disheartened and did not know what to do next. About ten minutes later, to our amazement, six young boys came wandering in, out of the darkness. "We are here for the Bible study" they said. We were so excited! The boys sat in a small, dark room with a few small candles providing light, as we read the story of Jesus' birth to them and let them color pictures of the Biblical account. It was the first time most of them had ever used a crayon.

The six boys who attended our first Bible study

That night we went to bed on a spiritual high. How amazing that God would allow us to share in this incredible opportunity! Imagine if we had followed common sense and returned to Conakry that day. As we were getting our stuff together to leave the next morning, we had another, even more shocking surprise. A couple high schools girls and the one of the chief's sons came up to our house. They said, "We are here for the Bible study." You are a little late, is what we were thinking. They continued, "We were at the mosque, and they announced that you were having a Bible study here." We could not believe our ears! They announced our Bible study at the mosque! Surely this was a mistake. I can't imagine "Come hear about Jesus from the Christians" being one of the bulletin points at the Islamic place of worship. Needless to say, we sat down with them as well and shared the stories of Jesus. I also sat with the chief's son and read the Bible with him. He had been trying to learn English, so we read some verses in Susu and then read the same verses in English.

On our way out of town we stopped by to tell some leaders that we were heading back to the capital. They confirmed that our Bible study truly was announced after prayer at the mosque. "We are sorry more students did not come to your house." Apparently, the person who made the announcement forgot to mention where we were located. I guess we will need to make sure they have all the details for any future announcements!

Reading the Bible with Pepe and the chief's son

April 19, 2008

The first two days in Mambia were centered on how to make our house livable – how to make my life comfortable. I was so frustrated, working so hard, at something that would take a lifetime to do. When we realized that we had wasted the first two days and had done no ministry, we changed our focus. That third day was the first day that we did ministry. And although we still had the bats and the ball tree, we had the satisfaction of sharing the gospel...not to live comfortably in Mambia, but rather to see souls come to Jesus. When you're doing ministry, it makes the sleepless nights worth it.

◆◆◆

YOUR SEARCH...

What are some things you do to provide a comfortable lifestyle that might be time better spent elsewhere?

List some benefits and drawbacks of having a comfortable life.

If you have been spending valuable time on the wrong goals, ask God to give you eternal perspective so that you can focus your time on things that matter.

"Therefore we do not lose heart. Though outwardly we are wasting away, yet inwardly we are being renewed day by day. For our light and momentary troubles are achieving for us an eternal glory that far outweighs them all. So we fix our eyes not on what is seen, but on what is unseen, since what is seen is temporary, but what is unseen is eternal."
- 2 Corinthians 4:16-18

CHAPTER NINETEEN
GOD IS ON THE MOVE

Despite the difficulties of our first extended stay in Mambia, we were eager to return and continue teaching the Bible. Due to a military coup in the country, however, our future trips to Mambia became more sporadic and unpredictable. We could not commit to travel due to the uncertainty of roadblocks and regular gas shortages. The ability to move about freely and without worry is another thing that we had taken for granted after living in America for many years.

During one of our stays in Conakry, while we waited for things to calm down, Jenn walked down the street with the kids to visit a friend with the American Embassy. While she was there, I sat outside our apartment on the balcony and watched the never-ending action that took place on the busy street below. Suddenly, I heard a lot more commotion than usual and saw hundreds of people running and screaming. As I watched closer and listened intently, I realized that there was gunfire coming from up the road and that people were running for their lives. When the seriousness of the situation hit me, I became terrified with the possibility that Jenn might be walking towards the apartment with our children at that same time. I frantically dialed her phone number in an effort to warn her to stay put. Unfortunately, she did not answer her cell phone. For a few brief moments, I debated whether I should leave the apartment and attempt to find her. Before I could make that choice though, she called back saying that she had not yet left our friend's home. Aware of the danger, she remained there until everything had returned to normal. It was a scary situation but once again God had everything under control.

The military coup made for no shortage of unusual stories. Because of the shootings and theft of the military, we were often told to stay in our houses. Stores and markets were closed in the middle of the day. Gunshots could be heard ringing out in the night. After a few weeks, there finally seemed to be a peaceful resolution to the volatile situation. Eager to get back out to Mambia, I drove to the first gas station that I could find open. There were four pumps and large lines to each one. Resolved to get gas that day, I took my spot as the tenth car in one of the lines. My vehicle had gas but I needed to fill a large container with gas so that we could keep our generator running. After about an hour of slowly inching forward, a man yelled something to me about not being able to get any gas. Being confused by what he said, I approached him to get clarification. He asked me if I had a container for gas and then told me to give it to him. Cautiously, I handed him the container and watched as he walked to the front of the line to fill it. The man at the first pump told him that he could not fill it there, so he went to the next one and they filled it for him. I told him thank you very much and then got in my car to drive away. As I was leaving, I noticed that no one else was pumping. Suddenly everyone else at the station got in their cars angrily and began leaving. All the pumps had just run out of gas! Praise the Lord for this angel who helped me to get the much needed gas!

"There was a loud cheer from those gathered as the clean, cool water came rushing out."

Subsequent trips to the village saw some exciting growth for our little Bible study. The small classroom was no longer big enough for the increasing number of students. We had to move onto the porch once we had 10-15 kids showing up. When it continued to growing, we began building wooden benches and teaching them in the yard in front of the house. "I never thought they would come to a Bible study" said our translator as we finished our 5th nightly Bible study. It was a sentiment that we had heard before. "You can't do a Bible school in a Muslim village. No one will come." That was what another person had said before we first began the work in Mambia. It was those words that ran through my mind as I watched over 30 children shuffle off into the darkness that night. Each night we continued sharing the story of Jesus to these children, using a coloring book filled with scriptures in their language; scriptures that none of them had ever heard before. On that particular night, as we ended, a few boys spoke up and requested that I pray for them. They asked that I pray for their education, for the future of their village and that they would learn the truth. It is a prayer that we continue to pray even today. We continued to teach the bible to 20-40 children every day and additionally witnessed to others in the village as we had opportunity.

Bible study in the front yard

As planned, we were able to repair one of the broken wells. After replacing all the pipes and parts, we grabbed the pump handle with the chief and, together, pumped until the water came out. There was a loud cheer from those gathered as the clean, cool water came rushing out. "Ye bara fa!" they yelled as they danced in the street. "Water has come!"

March 11, 2008

"Ye bara fa!" the people said. "The water has come" said the people of Mambia as their first well was finally working again. It was a long and exhausting day, but very neat and fulfilling. We are so happy to have fixed the well. The ladies danced. Paul, the chief and I pumped water. Paul spoke about Jesus providing living water. It was a cool day. Very neat to be a part of it.

Pumping well water with the chief

After that project, we began working on our second project which was to hand dig a new well. Three Muslim men were hired for the task. As was customary for them, they asked if they could sacrifice a chicken before breaking ground to insure their safety! Politely, we asked them to refrain from this and told them that we would ask God to protect them instead. They accepted and began digging a well without following the usual custom. Although they did stay protected, unfortunately we were not able to complete the project according to plan. The men digging reached very solid rock, perhaps granite, which could not be cut by hand. We discovered from this process that any wells in Mambia would need to be drilled rather than dug.

One day during our time in Mambia, I took the kids on a walk up the hill behind our house. There we met a man, his wife and their four children. Immediately we were struck by the condition of the man. Both of his legs were shriveled and useless. The man would scoot along the ground with wooden handles while his legs dragged lifelessly behind him. A few days later, we returned with Jenn and our translator to visit the man. Through the translator, we discovered that about 20 years earlier, he had been climbing a tree and fell out, breaking both of his legs. Since there was no one around to help him, his legs never healed properly and they became completely useless. We also learned that he and his wife originally had nine kids but five of them had died! The death of children is, sadly, so commonplace in these villages. We gave him and his family some Christian materials, some fruit and rice. After that, we brought him some water from the well we had repaired.

It was quite an eye-opening experience, as we saw the difficulty this man faced just in trying to provide for his family each day. As our vehicle struggled to make it up the washed out, steep, dirt road with 2 containers of water, it was impossible to imagine how his 14 year old daughter, 10 year old boy, 8 year old twins or his wife would manage to make it up this hill on a daily basis with water, that is so essential to drinking, cooking, and cleaning. It dawned on us that there were probably many more families just like this living in the hills all around us. I would also be willing to bet that many of those families have never heard the good news about the sacrifice of Jesus Christ. After repeated trips to meet with his family and witness to them, the "man on the hill" became the first person in Mambia to confess the truth of the gospel.

As the ministry grew, we began to wonder if God might also be using us to raise up local Christians to be missionaries in their own country. At the same time, we also began pondering our return to the States. We desired to be home but were not sure when the right time would come. One of the pivotal components that needed to be in place before we considered moving back, was feeling confident that we had someone who could continue the ministry in our absence. It became abundantly clear that God was raising up Pepe for this very purpose. He had proven his character to us on numerous occasions and his love for the Lord was evident in everything he did. While we saw God working in Pepe's life, helping him see the vision was another story entirely. I asked Pepe one night, if he would consider moving from his home in Conakry, out to the village to oversee the work that we had started. After thinking about it and discussing it for some time, he regretfully informed us that it was not something he was prepared to do. He had a home and a good job in the city where much of his family lived. "Village life is hard" he told us matter-of-factly. He was definitely preaching to the choir with that one! About one week later however, Pepe brought the discussion back up. "I've been praying about this and I think the Lord wants me to move out here and oversee the ministry." It was an answer to our prayers as well, and we began to pray that God would reveal the timing to us next.

YOUR SEARCH...
What experiences do you have in another country or culture?

What are some things that you think you or Americans in general take for granted?

Take some time over the next week or two, to keep a list of all the things you are thankful for but often take for granted.

"Be joyful always, pray continually, give thanks in all circumstances; for this is God's will for you in Christ Jesus."
- 1 Thessalonians 5:16-18

CHAPTER TWENTY

IT'S NOT GOODBYE

As the summer of 2008 approached, I learned that my siblings were planning a family reunion in July. It made sense to plan a return trip to California in order to be home for that. The reunion, however, fell apart and I began to think that maybe we should stay in Guinea longer. We considered staying at least another month or two and perhaps more. After all, it seemed like there was still so much work to be done. Was it really wise to leave someone in charge of the ministry when we had only spent time with him off and on for less than a year?

Jenn and I really began to struggle and pray through this. She believed that we should leave in July. I, on the other hand, was just not sure. We committed to each other that we would pray with an open mind and let God direct us. As time went on, I still had not felt any specific direction from the Lord, while Jenn began to feel more sure that we were supposed to return to the States. Because I still had not received clear direction from God, I made a choice to defer to her. We began looking for airline tickets. I decided that purchasing tickets could be like setting a "fleece" before the Lord. If God really did want us to return to California, He could open the doors as we planned our travel. The least expensive tickets, all the way into November, were on July 4th. "Okay" I said. "Let's buy them." I had another condition though. We were buying from a website that I had never used before and there was always a chance that the tickets would not be issued for some reason or another. (It had happened to me before.) I told Jenn that if this were the case, then we would believe that God had a different plan for us. I made the purchase online just before we headed out to Mambia for the week.

Shortly after arriving in Mambia, we got a call from Jenn's mom. Her mom said that our credit card company had called because they had put a stop on our card due to some unusual charges. Jenn was in turmoil. It seemed like we would not be returning in July, but there was no way to know until we returned to Conakry at the end of the week, since we had no internet in Mambia.

"I had quickly forgotten that it was never my ability to begin with."

In spite of the stress that had been caused regarding our plane tickets, we had an amazing time that evening at our nightly Bible study with the kids. As we finished the lesson time, an unknown man walked up to our Bible study from out of the darkness and began say all sorts of strange things. I confronted

~ 146 ~

him by asking him if he had heard of Jesus Christ. He said that he had and then began talking about how he was a good person. A strange feeling of power came over me and I felt like I was supposed to be bold and direct with this man. I told him that he was a liar and that his heart was wicked. I told him that the only way he could have victory over his problems was by accepting Jesus Christ. I asked him if he wanted to accept Jesus, and to my surprise, he said "Yes!" Without any direction, he came close and knelt in front of me. I laid hands on him and prayed for him. All this happened while about ten or fifteen of the kids stood around us and watched. It was absolutely amazing! After the prayer, the man disappeared into the darkness and we never saw him again.

As soon as this strange encounter had ended, my phone rang. It was the travel agent whom we purchased the tickets through! They were calling from Florida. Now mind you, it was often impossible to receive calls in Mambia because of poor cell reception. In addition, I have no clue how they got my cell number! They were calling to tell us that they had our tickets and that they just needed an address to send them to! It was a confirmation to me that God's timing was perfect and though I did not understand, He had His reasons. For Jenn, it was a sweet blessing from the Lord that He allowed her to sleep that night in peace, knowing that everything had worked out.

May 14, 2008

We arrived in Mambia yesterday. Unfortunately, it was very eventful. Selah threw up in the taxi twice on the way. The taxi had twelve people in it! Shortly after we arrived, my mom called to say that our credit card company had put a hold on our tickets. Ugh! I had to call the company asking them to please release the hold on the tickets, but I don't know if they will. I'm so anxious to know. I can't believe I have to wait six days before I find out if I'm really going back to America on July 4th. Although I hate being in this place of uncertainty, it's also good to trust in God. He loves me and knows what's best for me and I do trust Him. It's a good lesson. Oh, I pray that those tickets went through. Please Lord, I beg...

May 15, 2008

A man came to Bible study tonight. He wanted new life in Jesus. Paul and Pepe prayed for him and he accepted Christ. Awesome! Then, thirty minutes later, a lady with the travel agency called us in Mambia and said we got the tickets. They just needed an address to mail them to because they can't do e-tickets. Yeah! We got the tickets, but even more cool is God's confirmation and love for us. Hardly anyone gets ahold of us in Mambia and, since when do travel agents call? They usually just email. They especially don't call *people in African villages. It is so difficult to get a hold of us. It was like we did what God wanted us to do. A man needed Christ and Paul shared the truth with him and he accepted. Now we could go home. It was incredible and it was a great confirmation for us. God is awesome – so powerful and so loving.*

One of the struggles with leaving Guinea, was not knowing what would become of the ministry that had begun there. Thankfully, God had blessed us with an amazing companion in Guinea. Pepe was such a humble, hard-working man who was passionate about bringing glory to God. It was so encouraging to know that he would be leading this ministry in our absence and yet so difficult to leave him to oversee it. I knew how inadequate he felt and unprepared for all that he was agreeing to. I really wanted to be there with him. Perhaps it was another way for God to show His power that we were going home after only one year. In my pride, I battled the thought that the ministry would not be able to continue without me. I had quickly forgotten that it was never my ability to begin with. What better way for God to continue working, than by taking another "unqualified" servant and letting him take a step of faith.

After some very painful goodbyes and promises of a coming visit, we boarded our plane for America. On the evening of July 4th, we celebrated America's independence by watching the entire country explode in a display of light and color from our plane window. We celebrated our own moment of freedom too. Freedom to experience the joy, peace and fulfillment that comes from leaving all, to follow Christ. Freedom to sacrifice and put the lives of others above our own. God's work would continue in Guinea...and in us.

YOUR SEARCH...
Which things in your life are trying to hold on to tightly and keep control of?

How might God be calling you to let go of those things in order for Him to receive glory?

Make a list of changes you would like to see in your life and in the lives of your loved ones. Begin to pray that God would bring about change in His time and His way.

"Trust in the Lord with all your heart and lean not on your own understanding; in all your ways acknowledge him, and he will make your paths straight." – Proverbs 3:5-6

CHAPTER TWENTY-ONE
MANY HAPPY RETURNS

Upon our return home, we were faced with a very painful decision. Would we continue to be a part of the church in Bakersfield that we had spent years serving at and where many of our friends were still attending or was it time for us to move elsewhere? I had hoped we would be able to continue being a part of it, but I was unsure if it was the right thing to do at this time. We prayed fervently that God would show us what to do. It was our desire to inspire others to step out in faith and, perhaps to join us on a short term trip to Guinea.

Despite this, we had also come to realize that our philosophy of ministry did not align with the church leadership. It was apparent that regular attendance there would create a rift and perhaps division among the members. That was not our desire. We loved the church and the people there. We knew that the church was rooted in the Word of God and that many lives were being impacted by their ministry. In my heart, I knew it would be better for people to assume the worst of us, than for us to become a stumbling block to others. Jenn agreed to attend the church on our first Sunday back, as a way of testing the waters. We desperately wanted it to work. I was praying for something miraculous. Unfortunately, the service just confirmed what we had been feeling. Our relationships had changed and our priorities had shifted. Though it did not go as I had hoped, we both walked away that day knowing that God was clearly moving us on.

As often happens, God used this difficult separation to unveil more opportunities for ministry. Through this process, God lead us to a small church and specifically to a man named John. His church was just starting out, and they were passionate about missions. Instantly, our hearts were united. We began to serve where we could and made new friendships. It was not long before our relationships led to discussions of Guinea. The church was excited. Not only did they want to support us, they wanted to return with us. As I have mentioned, it was our desire to take teams back to Guinea, so that others could see what God was doing and perhaps develop God's heart for the lost as we had, so this was definitely an answer to prayer.

"Here we were in a Muslim village, being welcomed to teach the Bible to their children and now given land to do so with."

In July 2009, one year after leaving the work in Mambia, we took a team of seven others, besides ourselves, to visit the ministry in Guinea. The first day in the village brought tears to our eyes. Our van arrived in Mambia and pulled over on the side of the road. There was a large group of people there waiting for us. In the center was a choir of students who began to sing as we exited the vehicle. Our entire team was then escorted into a building just off the road. What we saw blew us away. Inside this building, was not just the six kids that we began a Bible study with back in February 2008, nor was it just the 30-40 kids that we had attending by the time we left in by that July. Inside this building were 81 students who were now attending our English Bible school in Mambia!

In addition to the students, it seemed like the entire village was there. We sat up front next to the chief, the Sous-Prefe, the Imam and the other officials of the village. The students sang worship songs and Pepe lead the welcome. We received a sheep and two chickens as a gift and were told once again that we could do whatever we wanted here in Mambia. They said we had left our home in America, and we were now at home in Mambia. At the end of the "program" they said they would give us land to build our Bible school on. They led us up a hill to a beautiful plot of land which was about 2 ½ acres in size. It was amazing! We were in awestruck by the power of God. Here we were in a Muslim village, being welcomed to teach the Bible to their children and now given land to do so with. On that day, I felt so assured that we had made the right decision to return to California. There was no way we could take any credit for what had been going on in Mambia. Sure, our initial move there was necessary to open the doors for this ministry, but we really did not need to stay there to have it flourish. God had it under control all along. He truly is an amazing God and so powerful beyond what we could even imagine.

Although I was excited to be the proud owner of almost three acres of land in Guinea, I really did not know what to do with it. "Build a school," you say? How was I supposed to do that? It had taken us months to raise enough money to buy a $1500 plane ticket to visit and now they wanted me to build an entire school! Once again, I had missed the point. It was not I who was being asked to build a school. It was God. He was just asking me if I was willing to be the vessel. For the moment, I concealed my doubt as good as I could and thanked them for the generous gift. As a group we stood together in a circle and prayed for God's will to be done. If He wanted us to build a school there, then He could make it happen!

As if all this was not enough, something else miraculous had taken place while we were gone. The village had given Pepe their old mosque to teach the students in! They were building a new one next door and allowed him to use this old building to teach the students on a daily basis. During our week stay in Guinea, we led a vacation Bible school program with the children that attended the Bible school. We acted out Bible stories, tie-dyed shirts, played games and showed the Jesus film in Susu, which is the local language. At that time, the Susu people did not have the Bible in their language, but they did have the Jesus film. We draped a white sheet over the Islamic symbol painted on the wall of the mosque and turned on the portable projector that we had brought for this purpose. About two hundred people gathered inside the room and when there was no more space inside, they stood outside peering through the open windows. Their eyes were glued and their mouths were shut as they watched the adaptation of Luke's gospel. For many of those that did not attend the Bible school, this was the first time they were able to hear the story of Jesus Christ. This was their first exposure to the gospel. It reminded me of the scene in Mark where the people crowded every space possible just to get a glimpse of Jesus.

"So many gathered, that there was no room left, not even outside the door, and He preached the word to them."
– Mark 2:2

Another incredible experience from that trip was being able to baptize five people. We did not even think we would get to be a part of baptisms while we were there because it is such a huge step for them to take in a Muslim village where they put themselves in risk of persecution. However, we were able to baptize four local people as well as one of our own team members. As we went down to a nearby river for the baptisms, the other Bible school students that were with us, led us in worship songs. We stood there singing praise songs while onlookers watched these people get baptized. Suddenly it began pouring rain as well. The entire spectacle was so surreal. The beautiful scenery of the river, the songs of soulful worship, the rain pouring down and the public expression of faith from those being baptized, combined to make one of the most amazing moments I have ever experienced!

River baptisms

Over the next few years, we continued to make regular trips back to Guinea. Each trip that followed, left us even more amazed at what God was doing. Through generous donations, we were able to begin work on our new land. God used so many people, all with their own stories and promptings. One such family, had experienced great tragedy and decided to turn that into an opportunity to see God glorified. Shortly after we moved back to California, we met a woman from the church we began attending. At the time, her husband had cancer and in January of that following year, he passed away. Her twenty-year old son was hoping to visit Africa with us, but was unable to, due to his health. Unfortunately, he too had been fighting cancer. Only seven months after his father died, he also passed away. His sister however, was able to attend that year and his mother accompanied us the following year. To honor the memory of these two men, this wonderful woman not only provided for a well, but also contributed greatly to the school.

There have been many others who gave selflessly and repeatedly to provide for our teachers, minister to orphans, build wells and construct buildings. To this day we are extremely grateful for their time and sacrifice, and we know that we could not have done it without them! I truly believe that when it comes to the kingdom of God, one person's job is no more important than anyone else's. Every part is important and vital to the work. In May 2010 we finished drilling our third well, this time on the land of our future school. In the summer of 2011, we began construction on what would later become a seven-room schoolhouse.

In the midst of amazing blessing and growth, there were undoubtedly trials and tribulations as well. One of the most heart-wrenching things we had to deal with took place in July 2011. Shortly after one of our trips to Guinea, I received a call from Pepe letting me know that his only son, Ibriham, had passed away the night before. They were not sure what went wrong, but he became sick and then died very suddenly. He was less than two weeks away from his seventh birthday. It was a devastating loss and being so far away made it even more painful.

Despite the trials, God continued to do miraculous things. We had even been asked by a nearby village to begin another Bible school there. We began doing that and quickly had over a hundred students in attendance. Another miracle was regarding getting the necessary approval to teach students at our schools. During our time away, the little two-hour Bible school and English class had now become two, full-day, multiple subject schools and those in charge were taking notice. The public school teacher in the second village complained to the authority because he was losing his children to our school. The government came in and closed our schools temporarily. They needed things to be done legally.

More than happy to oblige, we filled out the paperwork and submitted our application. The educational director however, needed to meet with me personally. During our trip in 2011, we arranged that meeting. The director informed us that she had not yet signed the approval because there was a problem with our school. We were teaching the Bible as our main curriculum and that was something the government could not be in support of. I was considering how I might respond to this when she suddenly just signed and stamped the approval paperwork and handed it back over! There were still some inspections that needed to take place before things became final, but we now had two schools in Guinea that were recognized by the government! It was something I never thought would be possible.

Our schoolhouse in Mambia

YOUR SEARCH...

Do you have a ministry in your life that you need to follow up on? How might you do that?

Are there people in your life who have made a difference but you have not yet shown your appreciation to? Who are they and what can you do to let them know that they have made a difference in your life?

Reach out to those who need encouragement. Be available for those who need assistance. Thank those who have poured into your life. God has not given up and neither should you!

"I thank my God every time I remember you. In all my prayers for all of you, I always pray with joy because of your partnership in the gospel from the first day until now, being confident of this, that he who began a good work in you will carry it on to completion until the day of Christ Jesus." – Philippians 1:3-6

CONCLUSION

A lot has happened since that call to go in the summer of 2006. We continue to take teams back to Guinea each year to continue and support the work which is growing, yet there have also been more trials. Besides losing Pepe's son, the man on the hill passed away and our missionary friend who helped us build the wells, also died suddenly. In March 2016, the worst recorded outbreak of the Ebola virus began in Guinea. Over 11,000 people in the surrounding areas lost their lives. All schools, including ours, were shut down for quite some time. After the outbreak, we restructured our ministry and closed the school in the neighboring village so that we could focus on building up the school in Mambia. In the summer of 2018, the chief who first welcomed us to the village passed away after years of deteriorating health.

Despite these and other struggles, we continue to be encouraged daily by the fruit of the ministry. There is now a beautiful, seven-room school house and housing for our teachers on our property. Not only have we built and fixed wells, we have also been able to install a solar pump and a water tower with the help of a friend from our church. For the first time, those at our school and in the surrounding area, now have running water. More people have come to the Lord. Our little church in the village is growing and for the first time, many people have a place to go to hear the gospel preached and Scripture read. More orphans, widows and sick are being cared for. God continues to receive the glory. In the summer of 2017, I finally bit the bullet and went through the process of obtaining non-profit status. We were so blessed that we received acceptance through the state and then through the federal government in just over two months!

We would love for even more miracles to happen. We are currently building a clinic where we hope to minister to the sick and wounded while also sharing the gospel and praying for them. Some of the members and leaders at the church in Mambia have begun taking a collection that could one day be used to make a church building. We also hope to build a guesthouse for visitors. We know however, that the projects and the ministry will continue to grow or come to conclusion depending on God's plan. It has never been about our ability or accomplishments. It has always and will continue to be about bringing glory to our loving God and mighty Creator. Regardless of what happens next, it has all been worth it. Even if it was just for the personal growth of me and my family, it was all worth it. If only for that first man who gave his life to the Lord or for the work done in Pepe's life, I would do it all over again. Every step of faith and every lesson learned along the way has been an opportunity to grow closer to God. As we discovered this small village in the middle of Guinea, West Africa, we were discovering more about our Savior.

March 8, 2008

I often wonder why the Lord chose us. Why He, the God of the universe, would reveal that He wanted us to move to Mambia. I am no spiritual giant. That's it...I'm an ordinary person and that's who God often chooses. Deuteronomy 4:33-35 says "Has any other people heard the voice of God...you were shown these things so that you might know that the Lord is God." He may have chosen me for several reasons, but one reason is sure – to show me that He is God. He is gentle, compassionate, powerful, a good listener, a consuming fire and bigger than this universe. He is love. He knows my name. I am engraved in the palm of His hand because he holds me so tight. He is my protector, my healer and my light. He is my all in all.

We hope that in reading this book you have realized that it is not really a book about Paul and Jennifer Prelle. It is a book about the love and power of God. The stories are testimonies of what He can do through an available and surrendered life. It is our desire that by reading this book, you too may be inspired to listen to that gentle prodding from the Lord, even when the odds are stacked against you. We hope that you might be willing to risk it all and take a step of faith in order to see the living power of God active in your life. Do not let your "faithfulness" to a specific ministry or your dedication to a location, be a cover for fear of the unknown and a desire for comfort. Should you attend a conference? Yes. Perhaps listen to another message online? Go for it! Engage in a Bible study? Definitely. Pick up an inspiring book by a renowned author? Sure. Do all of those! But don't neglect the most important part. Action. The time to go is now! Get up from that comfortable seat and open the door to a world hurting and in need. If nothing else, we could all use the exercise ☺

"Do not merely listen to the word, and so deceive yourselves. Do what it says." – James 1:22

For more information about the ongoing work in Guinea, follow us on Facebook or visit us online at...

www.onejeremiah.com

Or check here for older posts and updates...

http://missiontoguinea.blogspot.com

Made in the USA
Las Vegas, NV
02 February 2022

42933180R00104